Research Skills

Analysing, Researching and Presenting

Simon Moss

Research at Work
Analysing, Researching and Presenting
1st edition, 1st printing

Author
Simon Moss

Cover designer
Christopher Besley, Besley Design.

ISBN: 978-0-7346-0820-8 (print)
ISBN: 978-0-7346-2074-3 (ePDF)

Disclaimer

All reasonable efforts have been made to ensure the quality and accuracy of this publication. Tilde Publishing and Distribution assumes no responsibility for any errors or omissions and no warranties are made with regard to this publication. Neither Tilde Publishing and Distribution nor any authorised distributors shall be held responsible for any direct, incidental or consequential damages resulting from the use of this publication.

Published by:
Tilde Publishing and Distribution
PO Box 72
Prahran VIC 3181 Australia
www.tilde.com.au

Contents

About the author

Simon Moss (PhD Monash) is a Senior Lecturer in Psychology at Charles Darwin University in Darwin, Australia. Previously he was adjust Senior Lecturer in the Department of Psychology at Monash University in Melbourne, where he lectured in psychology, research design & method, and statistics & data analysis, and supervised students in leadership, emotions, integrity, personnel selection, and data analysis. He is also a registered psychologist.

Simon's primary research interest concerns how characteristics of organizations and societies, such as inequality of income or instability of jobs, influence the neural functioning—and ultimately the mood, creativity, intuition, engagement, honesty, and altruism—of individuals. His research also relates to the factors that promote honest, ethical, cooperative and dedicated behaviour in the workplace. Specifically, he is interested in the misconceptions of individuals that compromise wellbeing and performance.

Simon has published scientific papers in a broad range of disciplines, including creativity and problem solving, attention and concentration, facial expressions, psychological disorders, risk and safety, and stress management. He has also published a range of books and articles in the fields of leadership, personality, motivation, integrity, perception, attention, and stress.

Preface

Many students assume that learning about research will be boring and tedious. And they are usually right: Learning about research can be boring and tedious. Fortunately, to enliven this topic and to prevent relentless boredom, this book introduces a series of techniques.

Benefits of this book

First, this book does not comprise a series of formal principles about research. Instead, each chapter begins with some flawed research, usually conducted by one of the current affairs programs on Australian TV. Next, the chapter presents a set of procedures that students need to conduct, with reference to a hypothetical study on the association between income inequality and wellbeing. In addition, scattered throughout the chapter, are some fascinating scientific discoveries that are relevant both to research practice and to life in general. These examples are all designed to demonstrate important principles, enhance critical thinking, clarify the research process, and inspire the reader.

Objectives

Although the book is interesting, the objectives may seem rather monotonous. Specifically, after reading this book, you should be able to:

- Clarify the questions and hypotheses you would like to explore
- Review the literature on this research topic
- Conduct interviews, focus groups, surveys, and other techniques to collect data
- Analyse both quantitative and qualitative data
- Recognize and refute alternative explanations of data
- Report the research appropriately
- Write more persuasively, concisely, precisely, and engagingly.

Unlike some texts you may have read, this book is not only intended to help you pass the course. In addition, this book also imparts some skills that are vital to many jobs and careers. These skills include:

- The ability to uncover flaws in the arguments or opinions of other people

- The capability to persuade and to influence other individuals effectively
- The capacity to extract vital information from other people, by asking appropriate and often subtle questions
- The ability to derive suitable policies or recommendations from research and data
- The capability to write and to communicate effectively and fluently.

Chapter 1

Specifying a provisional topic and research question

On 9 September 2008, the current affairs show *Today Tonight* reported a story on the effect of food colouring on the behaviour of children. The show referred to a study that compared the academic progress of children who often eat foods with artificial colours to children who seldom eat these foods. The children who often eat these foods exhibited impaired performance on various tests of academic progress. The authors concluded that artificial colours seem to inhibit learning.

But, this research is not entirely convincing. Perhaps, some children—including children with learning difficulties—are particularly attracted to foods that are coloured brightly. So, if individuals experience a learning difficulty, they may be more likely to eat food that is bathed in colouring and additives. Learning difficulties may be a cause, and not a consequence, of consuming food additives. The aim and objective of most research is to distinguish the cause and the consequence. So, how can you decide on the preliminary aims and objectives of your research project?

Decide which topic to explore

In your course, you will need to conduct a research project. Sometimes, the instructor sets a specific topic, such as 'The causes of income inequality'. Sometimes, the instructor sets a broader topic, such as 'Inequality' or 'The economy'. Regardless, in most courses, you will be granted some choice over the topic of your research project.

Research discoveries

When people consider exciting possibilities and opportunities in the future, perhaps five or so years from now, they can more readily identify topics that will be inspiring (Torelli & Kaikati 2009).

The initial instincts of people are often misleading. However, after they distract themselves for 10 or more minutes, people often feel a powerful hunch over how to proceed. This hunch or intuition has been shown to be more accurate than initial instincts (Dijksterhuis 2004).

Procedure 1	Example
To decide which topics to explore, list some of your interests, passions, and fascinations.	Fred is interested in helping people and assisting communities. Because he has recently been traumatized at work, Fred has become more compassionate. He can empathize with people who experience fear and anxiety every day.

Procedure 2	Example
List some topics or fields in which you have acquired extensive knowledge.	Fred has acquired knowledge about accounting, banking and, finance. He works as a financial advisor and writes financial reports. He advices individuals and companies on how to invest effectively.

Procedure 3	Example
List some topics or fields that evoke strong emotions in you, such as anger or frustration.	Fred is very angry about the sharp increase in the remuneration of managers over recent decades. At his workplace, for example, the CEO was recently granted a pay rise of $2 million, despite a sharp decline in the revenue and profit of the company.

Procedure 4	Example
Uncover a topic or issue that you feel integrates many of these interests, skills, or concerns. Dedicate a few minutes to this exercise and then abandon this task for a while, perhaps half an hour. When you return to this exercise, a topic will sometimes emerge.	Fred distracted himself for 20 minutes. In particular, he contemplated his motivations to complete this course. First, as his manager warned, anyone in his workgroup who does not complete this course cannot be promoted to the role of senior advisor or receive a pay rise. Yet, Fred was aware that he was motivated by another goal as well—a goal that he did not really want to admit to anyone.
	After distracting himself for a while, Fred suddenly decided that he would explore whether inequalities in income within companies—that is, pronounced variations in wages across employees—might affect the wellbeing and productivity of employees.

Uncover interesting insights

After you have identified a possible topic to study, you should collect a diverse and interesting range of insights about this issue. You should not complete an exhaustive review of the articles or books on this topic; just read enough material to ensure that you have been exposed to many different perspectives.

Research discoveries

After individuals skim a diverse set of facts, their creativity tends to improve for a while. Their ideas are more likely to be original and insightful (Clapham 2001).

Procedure 1	Example
On the internet, read broad discussions on this topic, such as entries in encyclopaedias.	Fred visited the website www.google.com and entered 'Wikipedia income inequality' into Google. He clicked the mouse on the first site in this list. He then read this Wikipedia entry on income inequality. He knew this material may not be entirely accurate, but at least discovered some interesting insights about the causes and consequences of inequality. For example, as he discovered, in nations in which income inequality is low—and therefore people tend to earn similar wages—the rate of depression diminishes. Furthermore, in these nations, the rate of crime is low as well.

Procedure 2	Example
On the internet, read the summaries, sometimes called abstracts, of scholarly articles on this topic. After reading these abstracts, you will become familiar with the breadth of this topic and the major controversies.	Fred visited the website http://scholar.google.com.au/, called Google scholar. He entered the search terms 'income inequality wellbeing' into Google scholar. This search uncovered hundreds of articles. He clicked on the first article. The summary of this article appeared on the screen. According to this article, in countries in which inequality in income is rife—and some people are appreciably wealthier than other people—gambling is especially prevalent. He then continued to skim the summaries of about 100 other articles.

Integrate these interesting insights

After you read entries in encyclopaedias and skim many abstracts or articles, you may now be ready to formulate a preliminary research question. That is, you may be able to articulate a question or claim that you would like to assess and explore.

Research discoveries

After individuals deliberately restrict their ideas by imposing constraints—like restricting their suggestions to possibilities that begin with a vowel—their creativity improves. They can propose more interesting research questions (Pike 2002).

Procedure 1	Example
To develop a research question, first list the most interesting concepts that you learned about while skimming the literature	The most interesting concepts that Fred read about, apart from income inequality, was distrust, and resilience. For example, as he discovered, when income inequality in nations is pronounced, people are not as likely to trust each other. They perceive other residents as untrustworthy. Fred was fascinated by the concept of distrust. He had always trusted people in the past. He had even trusted his colleague at work, Barney. He did not realize that Barney did not warrant this trust.

Procedure 2	Example
List the most interesting theories that you learned about while skimming the literature. A theory is an explanation or account of various findings or events.	Fred read about social dominance theory. According to this theory, people who are granted authority like to maintain their power. They will, therefore, tend to adopt beliefs that defend their power and justify existing inequalities. They might, for example, claim that some

Procedure 2	Example
	communities are inherently superior to other communities. Because of their power, these beliefs become prevalent throughout society.
	Fred had been a victim of these beliefs. Barney was the youngest son of the CEO. He was regarded by the managers as special—as superior. His version of events was always believed. In contrast, nobody would believe Fred. They would never believe that he had been deceived by Barney.

Procedure 3	Example
Derive a research question that revolves around the relationship between the interesting concepts that, if possible, is consistent with the theory. Concepts that vary across people or settings, such as inequality of income or anxiety, are called variables.	Fred initially posed the question 'Does inequality of income evoke anxiety in individuals'. He then decided to restrict his emphasis on inequality in organizations rather than inequality in nations. He felt that inequality in organizations could be addressed more readily than inequality in nations. He therefore posed the question 'Does inequality of income in organizations evoke anxiety in individuals'.

Procedure 4	Example
Distinguish between the likely causes and outcomes.	Fred decided that income inequality is likely to cause anxiety rather than vice versa. That is, income inequality is the cause and anxiety is the outcome.

Chapter 2

Completing a literature review

On 12 August 2006, *Today Tonight* reported a story called 'A passion for positive thinking'. The reported centred on Michelle Matthews, a former employee of Ansett who became unemployed, depressed, and impoverished after the airline collapsed in 2001. She realized that she will need a positive attitude to overcome this predicament and thrive again in the future.

Four years later, she is now the director of a flourishing publishing business—a business with a turnover of half a million dollars. She feels that her success proves the benefits of positive thinking.

Yet, this conclusion that positive thinking is beneficial contradicts many scientific discoveries. According to recent studies, the effects of positive thinking are more nuanced (see Davidson & Moss 2010).

For example, in one study, people were asked to repeat positive aphorisms to themselves, including 'I am a likeable person'. They were also instructed to describe their mood before and after they repeated these aphorisms. Many participants felt more dejected after repeating these phrases, especially if their self-esteem was low (e.g. Brinol, Petty & Barden 2007).

As this research, and many other studies, has shown, positive thoughts often contradict the doubts that many people feel about themselves. These contradictions evoke feelings of uncertainty, anxiety, or dejection. Many students also express opinions and articulate conclusions that diverge from past research. How can you prevent these oversights and ensure you have read the relevant research?

Uncover a breadth of sources: The role of books and databases

To learn about all the key insights and knowledge on your topic, two sources of information are invaluable: books and databases. Books and databases expose you to many other articles.

Research discoveries

People are reluctant to read books or articles that conflict with their opinions or beliefs, called the confirmation bias. This tendency is particularly common while people experience negative emotions, such as uncertainty or anxiety (Jonas, Graupmann & Frey 2006).

When people skim a book or article first, and then read this material carefully, they learn the information more effectively. Research shows that people generally underestimate the benefits of this approach (Meeter & Nelson 2003).

Furthermore, when people decide to skim a book rapidly, their mood tends to improve. The confirmation bias tends to subside (Pronin, Jacobs & Wegner 2008).

Procedure 1	Example
Use your library catalogue to uncover several books on your research topic. Complete this procedure more than once. Often, students reject a book because the title diverges from their expectations or preferences. Later, however, they realize this book could actually extend their perspective and improve their research	Fred entered the search term 'income inequality' in his library catalogue. The catalogue uncovered 30 books that fulfil this criterion. One of the books was called 'The Spirit Level: Why more equal societies almost always do better' by Richard Wilkinson and Kate Pickett. He decided that he would borrow and read this book. Another book was called 'Causes of changes in the distribution of family income in Australia, 1982 to 1997-98' by David Johnson and Roger Wilkins. Initially, Fred decided to reject this book—he was interested in the consequences, and not the

Procedure 1	Example
	causes, of inequality in income.
	But later, he decided this book could be useful. Perhaps the book could uncover other concepts that may be relevant to his research.
	Fred wanted to be thorough. He had not been thorough before. For example, he had believed Barney naively. Barney had told Fred to send his financial reports to the gmail account of the manager, john.smith@gmail.com. Fred did not realize he had been deceived.

Procedure 2	Example
Before skimming these books, imagine some inspiring consequences of completing an excellent research project. After forming these images, students tend to be more receptive to diverse information.	Fred imagined describing his important research to a panel of people while applying for a job. He imagined they were impressed by his research and, therefore, offered him a job in policy. He envisaged that he could now leave his job and escape his pain

Procedure 3	Example
Skim these books to unearth: - The diversity of causes and consequences of your key variables - The theories or accounts that explain why these causes or consequences are related to your key variables - The characteristics or conditions that affect these relationships - Other article you should read.	Fred skimmed a few books. He identified many causes of inequality in income, such as the decline of unions and the degree to which the culture values work over family. He also discovered many consequences of income inequality, including increases in crime, teenage pregnancy, and mental illness. The main explanations of these findings revolved around competition. Specifically, as income

Procedure 3	Example
In particular, to unearth this information, primarily read the first sentence of each chapter. Read the entire paragraph only when you do not understand the first sentence. Nevertheless, after skimming these books, perhaps read the most helpful book again more carefully	inequality escalates, people know that competitive behaviour, such as outperforming other people, could greatly enhance their wealth. They are not as inclined to be cooperative. Their relationships decline, and trust dissipates. Other scholars suggested that inequality in income provokes impulsive decisions. In particular, when incomes are unequal, people cannot as readily predict their wage in the future. Consequently, they focus their attention more on their immediate needs instead of their future goals. They choose activities that enhance their emotions now, such as alcohol consumption, often to the detriment of their future. However, Fred also discovered that inequality in income does not always provoke these complications. In some countries or organizations, changes in income are very gradual rather than abrupt. Residents feel that competitive behaviour will not boost their wealth. In these countries or organizations, inequality in income does not provoke as many problems. Finally, a list of articles, called a reference list, appeared at the end of these books. Fred identified some articles that could be relevant to his research.

Read the most credible sources: The role of refereed journals

Research discoveries

People tend to show a tendency called the truth bias. That is, they are more likely to believe a claim that is incorrect than doubt a claim that is correct. For example, they often believe flawed arguments in books (McCornack & Parks 1986).

Because of this bias, students should attempt to confine most of their reading to sources that are likely to be accurate rather than misleading. The most accurate sources are refereed journals—periodicals that are like magazines but include only articles that have been reviewed and accepted by experts in the field. The articles in these journals are more likely to provide sound and valid research and reviews.

Procedure 1	Example
Besides books, you also need to identify which databases you can use to uncover relevant articles. Your instructor will usually tell you which databases are relevant to your topic and accessible to students. Examples include ■ 'Business source complete' for business or marketing students ■ 'Econlit' for economics students ■ 'Computer database' for IT students ■ 'Criminal justice abstracts with full text' for criminology students ■ 'AGIS plus text' for law students ■ 'Factiva' for students who need to search Australian newspapers ■ 'Australian public affairs	Fred decided that he would use Econlit and PsychInfo. He entered 'income inequality' as well as 'health', 'wellbeing', 'trust', 'resilience', 'competition', or 'impulsi*' as keywords. Note the asterisk in 'impuls*' implies that Fred was interested in any keywords that begin with 'impulsi', such as impulsive and impulsivity. He then specified an option that limited the search to refereed articles only. This procedure uncovered about 100 relevant articles in refereed journals.

Procedure 1	Example
information service' for social work students, and • 'PsychInfo' for psychology students If possible, limit the search to articles that appear in refereed journals.	

Procedure 2	Example
Sometimes, you can access the relevant articles from the database. On other occasions, you might need to locate these articles yourself.	Fred read the summary or abstract of these 100 articles. He then decided to read about 30 of these articles in more detail. While searching the database, he could then access 15 of these articles by simply pressing a link. He could then access the other articles by using an online library catalogue and then locating these journals in the library.

Collect facts and figures: The role of reports

Research discoveries

Readers are more likely to believe any claim that can be imagined vividly or understood easily (see Lev-Ari & Keysar 2010). Reports that include some precise facts or vivid case studies, therefore, are more likely to be rated favourably.

An excellent literature review will usually include some intriguing statistics or case studies. A report about inequality in income, for example, might emphasize that 'In Singapore and the UK, the richest 20% of individuals earn almost ten times the income as the poorest 20% of individuals. However, in Japan and Sweden, the richest 20% of people earn only four times the income as the poorest 20% of people.' Alternatively, the report might describe a case study in which, during a job interview, a person was offered an executive role and told the wage would be 2. The person assumed the wage was $200 000, accepted the job, but actually discovered the wage was $2 million.

Unfortunately, on the internet, many claims are exaggerated. So, to collect interesting but true statistics, confine your searches to reliable sites, such as the Australian Bureau of Statistics. This site presents a series of reports on a variety of topics, including the economy, health, education, and demographics. Similarly, to collect interesting but true case studies, confine your searches to reputable newspapers, either online or in paper, as well as sites that demonstrate how they substantiate their claims.

Procedure 1	Example
Uncover some interesting statistics from the Australian Bureau of Statistics, the CSIRO, or other credible research bodies.	Fred decided to enter 'Australian Bureau of Statistics income inequality' into Google. He uncovered some interesting statistics about the distribution or diversity of income across Australian households.

Procedure 2	Example
Find some intriguing case studies from credible sites. You could, for example, read the reports of institutions or companies that are sponsored to undertake qualitative research—research that usually involves interviews and focus groups. In addition, you could use databases that summarize newspaper articles, such as 'Factiva' or 'Newsbank newspapers'. Finally, you could visit sites that present validated stories and cases, such as snopes—a website that assesses the validity of common stories and legends.	Fred decided to enter 'Income inequality The Age' into Google. He also skimmed the information at snopes, located at www.snopes.com. Neither of these activities, however, uncovered any case studies on inequality. Nevertheless, Fred enjoyed this site. He liked how this site evaluates whether common beliefs and myths are true. He wished that his managers had questioned their beliefs as well—especially the belief that Fred did not complete any reports in the previous month.

Procedure 3	Example
When you transcribe past literature, indicate whether a piece of information is a quote, research finding, or opinion. You may include other codes as well, such as whether this source could be updated.	When Fred read the article that was written by Shigehiro Oishi and two other authors, he transcribed the quote 'One of the most profound social changes in the United States over the last 40 years has been the growing income inequality among social classes'. Fred recorded the page number 1095. He also inserted a Q alongside this sentence to indicate this extract was a quote. Furthermore, this article reported a study that showed trust diminishes in the US during the years in which inequality in income increases. Fred inserted an F alongside this sentence. The F represented the word finding. Finally, Fred was aware that some articles, such as entries in Wikipedia, are sometimes updated. Fred inserted a U alongside information that he collected from these articles. To ensure his arguments were not obsolete, Fred planned to check these articles a few days before submitting his report.

Procedure 4	Example
Record the authors, title, and other information about each book or article—enough information to ensure you can locate these sources again in the future. For books, this information should include the publisher and both the year and city in which the book was published. For articles, this information should include the source—such as the name and volume number of the journal—as well as the page numbers.	For the book written by Richard Wilkinson and Kate Pickett, Fred recorded the following information: Wilkinson, R., & Pickett, K. (2009). The spirit level: Why equality is better for everyone. London: Penguin. For the article written by Shigehiro Oishi and two other scholars, Fred recorded the following information: Oishi, S., Kesebir, S., & Diener, E. (2011). Income inequality and happiness. Psychological Science, Volume 22, pages 1095-1100.

Chapter 3

Finalising your research questions and hypothesis

On 10 July 2010, *Today Tonight* reported a story about the effect of nutrition and lifestyle on cancer. According to this report, Japanese people tend to live longer than individuals in almost every other nation. In addition, the incidence of cancer in Japanese people is very low. Nevertheless, after they emigrate to the United States, their longevity decreases and the likelihood of cancer increases.

According to scientists, the nutrition and lifestyle of Japanese people must somehow diminish the incidence of cancer. Japanese people drink plenty of green tea—a source of antioxidants—and consume plenty of fish—a source of Omega 3 fatty acids. They also meditate often. Some researchers have, therefore, concluded that antioxidants, Omega 3 fatty acids, and relaxation might protect individuals from cancer and other diseases.

Yet, these conclusions may be premature. Hundreds of other conditions and practices are specific to Japan, such as their music, art, climate, and terrain. Many of these conditions and practices could also affect the longevity and health of individuals. Even terrain has been shown to affect the community: As studies have shown, in flatter areas, violence and competition tend to subside (Henry 2009).

Researchers, therefore, need to be aware of alternative explanations to research findings; otherwise, these findings might be inconclusive. How can you design research projects that explore alternative explanations and prevent these complications?

Identify possible mechanisms: The mediators

The best research projects often examine why variables are related to each other. These research projects, for instance, might show that inequality in income diminishes trust. This decline in trust then might amplify anxiety. That is, income inequality → trust → anxiety

In this example, trust is called a mediator. That is, trust mediates the relationship between inequality in income and anxiety. Trust may the reason income inequality is associated with anxiety.

Research discoveries

When people experience a positive mood, their thoughts often shift to concepts that are remotely or indirectly related to each other. For example, in this mood, they can more readily determine whether or not three words, such as sore, shoulder, spell, are related to each other (Bolte, Goschke & Kuhl 2003). In this example, all three words are associated with the term cold.

When people decide to read information as rapidly as possible—not to fulfil some deadline but merely to challenge themselves—their mood improves (Pronin & Wegner 2006).

Procedure 1	Example
In a quiet and peaceful location, skim your summaries of past literature as rapidly as possible. Record all the variables you feel are associated your causes, outcomes, or both.	Fred decided to skim his summaries of the books and articles that he read. During this process, he recorded concepts that may be positively related to inequality in income, such as distrust, resentment, hope, and the motivation to excel rather than to cooperate. He also recorded concepts that may be positively related to anxiety, including distrust, workload, and the motivation to excel rather than to cooperate.

Procedure 2	Example
Identify the variables that are related to both your causes and outcomes. Some of these variables may be mediators.	Fred realized that distrust and the motivation to excel are associated with both inequality in income and anxiety. He therefore concluded that both distrust and the motivation to excel may be mediators.
	Initially, Fred was not certain why distrust may mediate the relationship between inequality in income and anxiety. Then, he experienced a sudden insight.
	Specifically, according to Fred, when income varies considerably across the employees of an organization, these individuals may be motivated to excel rather than to cooperate. They may not, therefore, trust one another. This distrust evokes suspicion and thus may increase anxiety.
	A week ago, Fred had experienced another sudden insight. But, this insight was not as uplifting. He had suddenly realized why he had been accused of inadequate productivity...

Identify possible qualifications: The moderators

Excellent research projects do not only examine why two variables are related to each other. Instead, excellent research projects often clarify when two variables are related to each other.

For example, inequality in income may not always promote a motivation to excel rather than to cooperate. Specifically, in organizations in which income primarily depends on experience, individuals do not feel they can increase their wage rapidly. In these organizations, inequality in income may not foster a motivation to excel. In contrast, in organizations in which income primarily depends on sales performance, individuals feel they might be able to increase their wage rapidly. Inequality in income should, therefore, incite a motivation to excel.

In this example, whether or not income depends on experience or performance is called a moderator. This variable moderates or changes the relationship between inequality in income and the motivation to excel.

Research discoveries
Some people tend to direct their attention to specific details rather than overarching patterns. Rather than focus on the shape of a face, they are more likely to notice a blemish, for example. Other people tend to direct their attention to the overarching pattern. If people focus on the overarching pattern, they tend to overestimate their knowledge about topics, called the illusion of explanatory depth (Alter, Oppenheimer & Zemla 2010). Because of this illusion, researchers often overlook moderators.

Procedure 1	Example
Consider the conditions or characteristics that could amplify or impede the relationship between the key cause and the mediators or mechanisms.	Fred reflected upon conditions or characteristics that could affect the association between inequality in income and motivation to excel. According to Fred, when the appraisals of performance are unfair, inequality in income may not elicit a motivation to excel and thus may not provoke distrust. In these organizations, people do not feel that excellent performance will attract a greater income. Therefore, the level of fairness might moderate or change the relationship between inequality in income and anxiety. Fred also deliberated over whether conditions or characteristics could affect the association between inequality in income and distrust. Initially, these thoughts were not as fruitful.

Procedure 2	Example
Consider the conditions or characteristics that could amplify or impede the relationship between the mediators or mechanisms and the key outcome	Fred deliberated over the conditions or characteristics that could affect the association between distrust and anxiety. After some contemplation, he decided that distrust may not always provoke anxiety.
	In particular, if employees tend to work independently, their distrust of one another may not be as likely to provoke anxiety. In these workplaces, because the employees feel independent, they are not as vulnerable to victimization. Distrust, therefore, may not translate into vigilance or anxiety.
	Overall, Fred concluded that fairness of appraisals and level of independence may moderate some key relationships. He decided that he may explore these variables.

Identify alternative explanations:
Direction of causality and spurious variables

In some research projects, the findings are misleading. That is, researchers will reach conclusions that are actually misguided.

To illustrate, suppose that researchers discover that inequality in income is associated with anxiety. That is, when incomes vary appreciably across the organization, employees tend to be especially anxious. This finding may not indicate that inequality in income provokes anxiety. Instead, researchers need to consider two alternative explanations.

First, anxiety may promote inequality in income rather than versa. That is, income inequality ← anxiety. The direction of causality—the direction of this arrow—may be the opposite to the assumptions of researchers. Perhaps, if managers are anxious, their decisions about pay rises are erratic. Some employees will receive pay rises. Other employees will not receive pay rises. Inequality in income may soar.

Second, inequality in income and anxiety might not affect one another at all. Instead, another concept or variable might affect both inequality in income and anxiety. That is, inequality in income ← consumer confidence → anxiety.

To demonstrate, when consumer confidence declines, and sales diminishes, organizations might offer exorbitant salaries to attract the best executives. Yet, because revenue has decreased, only executives will attract a large salary, and inequality in income will increase. Anxiety will as well because job security is threatened.

Research discoveries

Consider the barber paradox. A male barber shaves all men who do not shave themselves but nobody else. Does this barber shave himself? If the barber does not shave himself, then he must shave himself to follow this principle. If the barber does shave himself, then he must not shave himself to follow this principle. Both of these alternatives are impossible.

Interestingly, after people contemplate this scenario, or similar paradoxes, they become more willing to tolerate and embrace uncertainty or ambiguity (Miron-Spektor, Gino & Argote 2011). These individuals, therefore, are more likely to consider alternative explanations rather than form definitive conclusions.

So, in some nations or states, both inequality in income and anxiety will seem to be high. In other nations or states, neither inequality in income nor anxiety will be as high. These two variables, therefore, will seem to be related to each other. They will seem to affect one another. Yet, these two variables do not actually affect each other but are both influenced by another variable: consumer confidence. In this instance, consumer confidence is called a spurious variable.

Procedure 1	Example
For a few minutes, imagine your beliefs about the relationship between your key variables are incorrect. This exercise can both uncover important insights as well as increase your tolerance of uncertainty.	Fred assumed that inequality in income would increase anxiety. For a moment, he contemplated the possibility that inequality in income may actually decrease anxiety. That is, he reflected upon why inequality in income could foster calmness instead of anxiety.
	He considered the possibility that

Procedure 1	Example
	inequality in income could foster a motivation to excel and, therefore, could improve productivity. That is, employees may complete more work in a limited time. Therefore, they may leave earlier and spend more time with their family, diminishing their stress and anxiety.
	Indeed, Fred was aware that his preconceptions are often misleading. He had assumed, for example, that he had sent all his reports to the manager. But actually, emails send to john.smith@gmail.com were not received by the manager. Instead, these emails were received by Barney. Barney would then insert his name on these reports and then send the final version to the manager.

Procedure 2	Example
Consider the possibility your outcome is actually a cause and vice versa.	After the previous exercise, Fred began to feel excited by his research. He felt motivated to contemplate other complications and subtleties of his study.
	Fred attempted to mount several arguments to explain the possibility that anxiety might promote inequality in income rather than vice versa. Yet, after a while, he felt these arguments were unconvincing.

Procedure 3	Example
Identify variables—that is, conditions or characteristics—that could influence both your cause and outcome. This exercise uncovers spurious variables.	After his literature review, Fred was aware of several variables that could promote inequality in income: economic instability, ineffective unions, and a competitive culture. Fred was also aware of several variables that could provoke anxiety: economic instability, uncertain roles, and inadequate leadership.
	Fred realized that economic instability could foster both income inequality and anxiety. Economic instability, therefore, may be a spurious variable. When explaining his results later, he may need to consider this variable.

Develop your hypotheses

Finally, before you design your project, you may decide to formulate hypotheses. Hypotheses are specific predictions, derived from a particular theory or explanation. If the findings contradict the hypotheses, the theory or explanation may be incorrect. If the findings align to the hypotheses, the theory or explanation is more likely to be correct.

Procedure 1	Example
Skim the insights you derived after you contemplated mediators, moderators, and spurious variables. Summarize these insights to formulate hypotheses or predictions.	Fred formulated several hypotheses. 1. Inequality of income in organizations should increase motivation to excel. 2. Motivation to excel should increase distrust 3. Distrust should increase anxiety in employees 4. When the procedures are fair, the relationship between motivation to excel and distrust should be especially

Procedure 1	Example
	pronounced.
	5. When employees work independently, the relationship between distrust and anxiety should not be as pronounced.
	6. Economic instability should be related to both income inequality and anxiety.

Because of time constraints, you may not be able to assess all your hypotheses. Nevertheless, these hypotheses are still useful, as you will discover later.

Chapter 4

Designing questions for participants

On 8 August 2011, *Today Tonight* reported a story about which foods are most unhealthy. The story highlighted that many foods, such as kebabs, smoked salmon sandwiches, potato salad with egg, as well as pastas or rices with chicken are often contaminated with bugs. In addition, the report also emphasized that many foods—including Quiche Lorraine, pizzas, kebabs, baklava, and chicken biryani—are high in calories and therefore fattening.

Yet, one possible complication was not considered. To illustrate, many people may perceive a pizza as unhealthy. Therefore, after eating a pizza, they may be more likely to consume a salad, or some other healthy dish, later in the day. In contrast, people may perceive a chicken biryani as healthy. After eating this meal, they may not feel the need to consume a healthy dish later in the day.

So, a study that is merely confined to calories disregards many vital considerations. Foods that are high in calories may, sometimes, reduce the amount of fatty or unhealthy food that people consume later. This study should not have measured only calories. This study should have measured the effect of eating one dish on consumption later in the day.

As this example shows, many studies do not ask the right questions. How can you ensure the questions you ask people are appropriate?

Vivid and simple questions

Scholars have developed a variety of methods and approaches to examine research questions and to assess hypotheses. In some studies, researchers may observe people or ask individuals to complete various tasks. In many studies, however, researchers administer surveys, interview participants, or organize a panel of individuals, called focus groups. To conduct surveys, interviews, or focus groups, the researchers must design questions that assess the key variables: the causes, outcomes, mediators, moderators, and spurious variables. The most effective questions are vivid and easy to understand.

Research discoveries

If the questions in a study refer to vivid events and are easy to understand, the participants will devote more effort to their answers. They will perceive these questions as very important (e.g. Labroo, Lambotte & Zhang 2009).

Phrases that are repeated frequently tend to be perceived as easier to understand and, therefore, increase the motivation and concentration of participants (e.g. Nordhielm 2002).

An example of a question may be 'On a scale from 1 to 10, to what extent do you feel anxious'. In this question, the participants must specify a number. When participants need to specify a number, the data is often called quantitative.

An example of another question may be 'Why do you sometimes feel that people are untrustworthy?' In this question, the participants must express words instead of data. When participants need to express words, the data is often called qualitative.

Surveys often, but not always, generate quantitative data. Interviews and focus groups primarily generate qualitative data.

Procedure 1	Example
Initially, write a series of provisional questions as rapidly as possible. Do not evaluate or optimize your questions yet. If the data is quantitative, each question should relate to one of your variables. If the data is qualitative, each question should ask people to consider the causes or consequences of each variable.	Fred decided that he would like to generate both quantitative and qualitative data. To generate quantitative data, he quickly developed some preliminary questions that assess inequality in income, motivation to excel, distrust, anxiety, justice, economic instability, and competitive culture. He wrote 'On a scale of one to ten, to what extent do you feel that: ▪ In your organization, the

Procedure 1	Example
	incomes of employees are dispersed ■ Employees are motivated to excel ■ In this organization, distrust is common ■ Your colleagues are anxious ■ The procedures are just ■ The financial performance of your organization is unstable'. To generate qualitative data, he also quickly developed some questions that relate to the causes or consequences of these variables: ■ How would you feel if income differed more appreciably between employees and managers? ■ How you would you feel if you knew that your colleagues were more driven to succeed than to help one another? ■ Would you feel anxious if you did not trust your colleagues?

Procedure 2	Example
To refine these provisional questions, ensure each word is quite specific and unambiguous. That is, change words that represent a broad range of possibilities.	Fred was determined to resolve any ambiguities. After all, an ambiguity had ignited the conflict between himself and Barney. Several months ago, Fred had described Barney as well rounded. Barney, sensitive about his weight, assumed that Fred was referring to his plump body. For the next few days, Barney snubbed Fred.

Procedure 2	Example
	Fred felt the question 'The procedures are just' was not suitable. 'The procedures' could refer to a diverse array of possibilities. Instead, Fred developed several questions, each referring to a specific procedure. He wrote 'On a scale of one to ten, to what extent do you feel that: - In this organization, the procedures that are used to evaluate employees are fair and just - In this organization, the procedures that are used to decide which individuals receive a promotion are fair and just - In this organization, the procedures that are used to distribute the work are fair and just'.

Procedure 3	Example
If some of the questions are still ambiguous, rather than precise, compare the main premise to the opposite possibility.	Fred felt the question 'Employees are motivated to excel' is still imprecise. He decided to change the question to 'Employees are motivated to excel rather than to help one another'. That is, he compared this motivation to excel to the opposite motive—the motivation to help one another.

Procedure 4	Example
Use only common words.	Fred decided that he did not like the question 'In your organization, the incomes of employees are dispersed'. He felt that 'dispersed'

Procedure 4	Example
	is not a common word and, therefore, the sentence is not especially easy to understand. He changed the question to 'In your organization, the incomes of employees vary considerably from one another'.

Procedure 5	Example
Ensure that different questions refer to the same phrases.	Fred realized that only two of the questions refer to employees. Fred decided that other questions could allude to employees as well. Furthermore, other questions could refer to the phrase 'In your organization', such as: ■ In your organization, employees often distrust one another ■ In your organization, employees often seem anxious.

Procedure 6	Example
For surveys, besides the wording, the format is also important. Ensure the font is simple to read: The letters should be large and clear. Furthermore, ensure the questions are arranged in a logical order.	Fred recognized that two of the questions—' In your organization, employees often distrust one another' and 'In your organization, employees often seem anxious'—seem, at least superficially, to be related to each other. He, therefore, decided these two questions should appear consecutively.

Suitable prompts and examples

To ensure that questions are vivid rather than ambiguous, researchers often include prompts and examples. For example, the researcher might write 'The financial performance of your organization—such as the profit and revenue—is unstable'. In this example, the reference to profit and revenue is included to clarify financial performance. Similarly, the researcher might ask 'How would you feel if income differed more appreciably between employees and managers: resentment or anger, for example?' Regrettably, these examples and prompts can bias the responses of participants.

> ## Research discoveries
>
> The examples or prompts in questions can significantly bias people. In one study, some participants were asked whether they feel that Africa covers more than 5% of the landmass of Earth. Other participants were asked whether they feel that Africa covers more than 50% of the landmass. Next, all participants were asked to estimate the percentage of landmass that Africa covers. If participants had earlier been exposed to the 5% prompt, instead of the 50% prompt, they assumed that Africa covers a smaller area. The prompt biased their final estimates (Tversky & Kahneman 1974).

Procedure 1	Example
Sometimes, you may feel you need to include examples or prompts to clarify the question. In these instances, include one typical or moderate example or prompt. In addition, include two extreme, but opposing, examples or prompts.	To clarify the question 'How would you feel if income differed more appreciably between employees and managers', Fred first decided to include two examples or prompts, such as 'resentment or anger'. He then recognized that resentment and anger are too similar and could bias participants. Instead, he included one moderate example: 'unaffected'. Plus, he included two extreme but conflicting examples: 'anger' and 'hope'.

Barney had also demonstrated extreme behaviour. After snubbing Fred for several months, Barney was suddenly friendly. He invited Fred to lunch. He complimented Fred's clothes. Although initially relieved, Fred knew that something was awry... |

Time frame of questions

Besides including simple words and specific examples, another technique can be utilized both to ensure the questions are vivid and to prevent some biases. In particular, the questions should revolve around recent weeks or months instead of the distant past or future.

Research discoveries

When people reflect upon a recent occasion, instead of the distant past or future, their attention is directed to specific details instead of intangible concepts. Consequently, their responses may be more precise (Trope & Liberman 2003).

When individuals contemplate previous episodes in their life, such as their first job, they are more likely to recall their achievements and not as likely to remember their mistakes. Their memories, therefore, are biased (Croyle *et al.* 2006).

When employees begin a job, they usually plan to stay for several years. If they eventually decide to leave after only six months, they cannot usually remember their original plan. Instead, they believe they had always assumed they would leave within the first year. That is, people tend to presume, often incorrectly, their behaviours matched their plans (Pieters, Baumgartner & Bagozzi 2006).

Sometimes, people are asked to predict their emotions or attitudes in the future. They might be asked 'How happy would you feel if you received a huge rise in your salary next year?' In general, these forecasts are quite inaccurate. For example, people tend to overestimate the intensity of their emotions. In this example, they might predict they will be extremely happy but, actually, only experience mild joy, after receiving a rise (Wilson & Gilbert 2003).

Procedure 1	Example
Some questions refer to characteristics or conditions that may change across time, such as mood or share price. In general, these questions should imply or allude to a recent timeframe, such as the last week or month. These questions should all refer to the	Fred decided to update the question 'In your organization, employees often seem anxious' to 'In your organization, over the last month, employees seemed to be anxious'. He also updated several other questions, such as 'Over the last month, employees have been motivated to excel rather than to

Procedure 1	Example
same timeframe as one another.	help one another'. He did not update all the questions though. Some of the questions alluded to characteristics, such as inequality in income, that are unlikely to change over the year.

Specific questions targeting intractable problems

Research discoveries

Do you feel the statement '85% of attempted instances of rape are successful' is true? Do you feel the statement '15% of attempted instances of rape are unsuccessful' is true? These two statements are logically equivalent. Yet, people are more likely to believe the first statement is true. Statements that highlight a devastating issue are more likely to be believed (Hilbig 2009).

Sometimes, people cannot decide how to pose a question. Should they express a positive slant, such as 'How often do you feel content?' Alternatively, should they express a negative slant, such as 'How often do you feel anxious?' Subtle changes to the phrasing can translate into dramatic differences in the responses. When people are not certain how to express a question, two possibilities should be considered.

Procedure 1	Example
Sometimes, you might not be certain which of two or more alternatives you should include. In these instances, include both alternatives. You could ask the same people both options. Or you could ask some people one option and other people another option.	Fred wasn't sure whether to include the questions 'In your organization, employees often distrust one another' or 'In your organization, employees often trust one another'. Initially, he preferred the first option, then he was so sure. He decided, therefore, to ask all participants both questions. He knew these questions could actually generate incompatible responses. That is, some participants may feel employees often distrust each other but also feel the same employees often trust each other as well.

Procedure 2	Example
Sometimes, you are not certain whether you have phrased your questions appropriately. Whenever possible, rather than construct your own questions, administer established measures. That is, include measures that past research has demonstrated to be valid.	Fred consulted other studies that have examined the variables that he wanted to explore. He discovered that many studies use a measure called the PANAS—or the positive affect and negative affect scale—to gauge mood. That is, participants are asked to indicate the degree to which they feel various emotions, such as anxiety, happiness, sadness, and anger. In addition, he discovered that many studies use a measure to assess whether or not the procedures are just. Fred decided to replace some of the questions that he had constructed with these two measures.

Indirect questions

In general, when people answer questions about their attitudes or behaviours, they like to depict themselves favourably. Consequently, they often exaggerate the extent to which they are confident, capable, and cooperative. To illustrate, even if unconfident, they may claim to be confident while completing questionnaires.

Specifically, if the purpose or aim of some question is too obvious, the responses are often biased. In contrast, if the purpose or aim of some question can be concealed, this bias subsides. To conceal the purpose or aim of some question, researchers ask questions that only they, but not their participants, know offer some insight into the variable of interest — called an implicit or indirect measure.

Research discoveries

Rather than ask people 'Is your self-esteem high?', participants are sometimes asked 'Do you like your full name?' Studies show that people who like their name tend to perceive themselves as confident and capable. That is, their self-esteem is often, although not always, high (Gebauer, Riketta, Broemer & Maio 2008).

If people are asked 'Are you willing to pay a carbon offset', many people say 'Yes'. If asked 'Are you willing to pay a carbon tax', many people say 'No', even if both the carbon offset and carbon tax are defined using the same words (Hardisty, Johnson & Weber 2010). Incidental words, therefore, can significantly bias the responses of participants.

Procedure 1	Example
Using Google Scholar or some other database, search the literature to establish whether or not researchers have developed an implicit measure of the variables you want to examine. These measures are primarily utilized to generate quantitative rather than qualitative data.	Fred entered 'implicit measure income inequality' into Google scholar. He did not, however, uncover any implicit measures of inequality in income. He used the same procedure to uncover implicit measures of other variables. Eventually, he unearthed an implicit measure of motivation to excel.
	Specifically, a series of illustrations are presented. Each illustration represents one or two people performing some activity. A set of questions follow each presentation such as 'To what extent do you feel the people are trying to solve some work problem' or 'To what extent do you feel the people are trying to support each other'.
	The answers to these questions, apparently, offer some insight into the motivation of people. For example, participants who are motivated to excel will assume the people in these illustrations also share this motivation. They will presume these people are trying to solve a work problem rather than support each other.
	Fred was interested in these indirect methods. In one sense, he had been the victim of an indirect

Procedure 1	Example
	method. Rather than ostracise Fred overtly, Barney decided to act friendly but behave maliciously. Not only did he insert his name on the reports Fred had written, Barney also left some underwear in the boardroom. He then wrote Fred's name on the label. Fred was later accused of inappropriate behaviour at work.

Procedure 2	Example
If you want to generate qualitative data—that is, words rather than numbers—ensure your questions are open-ended rather than close-ended. That is, begin the question with words such as 'How' or 'Why' to elicit a diversity of answers.	Initially, Fred had planned to ask participants 'Would you feel anxious if you did not trust your colleagues?' But, he realized this question is close-ended. The only answers are yes and no. The answers cannot be diverse. Instead, Fred decided to ask 'How would you feel if you did not trust your colleagues?' If participants do not know how to answer, he could include a prompt like 'Anxious, unaffected, excited, or what?'

Chapter 5

Design methodology

On 5 October 2006, *Today Tonight* reported a story about the prevalent challenges of teenagers today, such as drug use and teenage pregnancy. To explore these challenges, Today Tonight conducted a focus group with a collection of teenagers, all of whom were between 16 and 17 years of age. The focus group was conducted to assess the frequency and severity of these issues.

These focus groups demonstrated that alcohol is readily available to teenagers. In addition, many of these individuals claimed they feel pressure to engage in sex, even before they may be ready. Yet, the focus groups, apparently, also uncovered another insight: Teenagers admit they feel a strong pressure to conform.

But, this admission highlights a complication. If individuals really do feel pressure to conform, then perhaps some of their answers during this focus group were not accurate. That is, perhaps they felt pressure to conform to the answers of other participants. They may have felt compelled to claim they can readily access alcohol. They may have felt obliged to pretend they have felt pressure to engage in sex. The researchers, therefore, may have overestimated the frequency or severity of these concerns.

Focus groups, although useful whenever researchers want to explore one topic in detail, should not be used to establish the frequency or severity of some issue. The responses are often inaccurate. How can you ensure the methods and approaches that you utilize are suitable?

Decide how to deliver the questions

Research discoveries

After men observe attractive women, their behaviour changes. Interestingly, they are more likely to behave rashly. They often choose actions that evoke pleasure now but regret later (Wilson & Daly 2004).

Questions that are asked by an attractive person may generate different responses to questions that are asked by an unattractive person. Therefore, when you decide who will deliver the questions—or how these questions will be delivered—you need to be thoughtful.

Procedure 1	Example
If you plan to administer a survey, you may be able to deliver the questions by email or text. Software and apps are available to fulfil this need, such as: ■ Survey Monkey: www.surveymonkey.com ■ Zoomerang: www.zoomerang.com ■ Fluid Surveys: fluidsurveys.com ■ My Survey Lab: www.mysurveylab.com ■ Survey Gizmo: www.surveygizmo.com ■ Survey Methods: www.surveymethods.com ■ Impressity (do a Google search) These packages tend to be cheap or even free. Most of these packages, including Zoomerang and Survey Monkey, offer a diversity of features. Many apps, such as TouchPoint, can be utilised to survey people by text message. Text messages enable researchers to apply a technique	Fred decided that he will conduct interviews first. At the end of these interviews, he will then ask the individual to complete a survey on paper. He felt, therefore, that he did not need to deliver the questions by email or text.

Procedure 1	Example
called momentary sampling. In particular, if they send questions by text, researchers can assess participants at different times of the day. Momentary sampling is especially useful to researchers who want to explore how various feelings or states, such as level of engagement at work, vary across the day.	

Procedure 2	Example
If the questions are delivered by email, text, or traditional mail, participants will not need to converse with a researcher. However, if the questions are asked in person, the participants will need to converse with a researcher. The attributes of this researcher can sometimes affect the responses of participants. To avoid this problem, if possible, ensure the same person questions all participants.	Unfortunately, Fred knew that he could not interview all the participants himself. His instructor had told Fred that he must collaborate with someone else. In particular, he was told to collaborate with Barney, who had also enrolled in this course. Actually, Fred wanted to collaborate with Barney. He could then initiate his revenge. Conceivably, both Fred and Barney could interview the participants at the same time. However, if Fred interviewed some of the participants and Barney interviewed the other participants, they would save considerable time. So, they decided to assign some of the interviews to Fred and some of the interviews to Barney.

Procedure 3	Example
If more than one researcher needs to deliver questions, some problems could unfold. In this instance, you	Together, Fred and Barney planned to interview 20 managers and 40 employees who are not managers.

Procedure 3	Example
could randomly allocate a researcher to each participant. Alternatively, you could ensure the each researcher interviews participants with the same profile on key demographics.	Fred decided to interview 15 managers and 30 employees. Barney would interview the other 5 managers and 10 employees. Importantly, the proportion of managers did not differ between Fred and Barney. In addition, both Fred and Barney ensured they interviewed the same proportion of males and females.

Standardize the setting

Research discoveries

People who sit in the centre of a room or table are more likely to be evaluated favourably than are people who sit on either side (Raghubir & Valenzuela 2006). After people are exposed to symbols that represent fast food, such as Colonel Sanders or the arches at McDonalds, their decisions about other matters become more rash (Zhong & DeVoe 2010).

Many other cues in the environment can affect the attitudes and preferences of people. Classical music elicits a preference towards expensive options. Pictures of clouds elicit a preference towards comfortable alternatives (Mandel & Johnson 2002).

People tend to be more honest when a subtle whiff of citrus, such as Windex, pervades the air (Lilenquist, Zhong & Galinsky 2010). However, they are less honest when the room is dim (Zhong, Bohns & Gino 2010).

When a questionnaire is attached to a heavy clipboard, participants are more likely to reflect upon the questions carefully (Jostmann, Lakens & Schubert 2009).

Subtle features of the environment can shape the attitudes and responses of participants. Although not always possible, researchers should ensure that all participants are exposed to the same environment.

Procedure 1	Example
When you need to choose the room or location in which to	Fred and Barney booked a room at their TAFE. The room was

Procedure 1	Example
conduct interviews, focus groups, or surveys, several principles should be followed:	moderate in size with a round table. They cleaned the room thoroughly and opened the blinds.
▪ Focus groups, if possible, should be assembled around round rather than rectangular tables.	
▪ Rooms should be relatively inconspicuous—simple in design but not too bleak. Any striking decorations and paintings can bias the responses of participants.	
▪ The room should be very clean. Cues that correspond to hygiene, including the smell of citrus, elicit honest answers.	
The room should be well lit.	

Experimental designs

In one study, all participants completed tasks in groups of three and were randomly assigned to one or two conditions. In one condition, the participants all received the same amount of money to complete these tasks. In the other condition, the amounts of money that each participant received depended on their performance. Finally, the participants completed a questionnaire, intended to assess the degree to which they trusted the other people in their group.

Compared to participants who received the same amount of money as one another, participants who received different amounts of money to one another were not as trusting. This finding indicates that inequality may provoke distrust.

In this example, two alternative explanations can be readily dismissed. First, nobody can argue that distrust provoked inequality rather than vice versa. That is, the direction of causality cannot be questioned.

Second, nobody can argue that a spurious variable, such as economic instability, influenced both inequality of income and distrust. These explanations are incorrect, because inequality was manipulated by the researchers rather than influenced by other variables.

Whenever participants are randomly assigned to conditions or settings, the design is called an experiment. The findings of experiments cannot be ascribed either to the opposite direction of causality or to spurious variables. Consequently, experiments are often heralded as the most informative design.

Research discoveries

Many studies have shown that extraverted people tend to experience more positive emotions, such as excitement, than introverted people. Nevertheless, these studies were not experiments. Therefore, some researchers argued that, perhaps, positive emotions elicit extraverted behaviour rather than vice versa.

Recently, however, an experiment was undertaken to explore this controversy. Some participants were asked to behave like an extravert. Other participants were asked to behave like an introvert. Next, their emotions were measured. People who acted like an extravert were more likely to experience positive emotions than people who acted like an introvert. These results indicate that extraversion does indeed evoke positive emotions (McNiel & Fleeson 2006).

Procedure 1	Example
To decide whether or not to conduct an experiment, consider whether or not you can feasibly manipulate the key cause in your research.	Fred decided that he could not feasibly manipulate income inequality—the key cause in his study. Although some past studies have manipulated income inequality, the procedure was costly and protracted. That is, the researchers needed to pay the participants various amounts of money after completing a task. Because Fred needed to complete his study with a limited budget, and within a tight deadline, he decided to measure, rather than manipulate, income inequality. So, he did not conduct an experiment.

Chapter 6

Implementing the research you designed

On 17 November 2011, *Today Tonight* reported a story on a machine that people can utilize to reduce their weight. The machine utilizes ultrasound to stimulate fat cells. These cells, therefore, gradually diminish in size.

Preliminary studies have shown this apparatus, called the Med Contour machine, does indeed reduce weight. That is, people who use the machine were more likely to report weight loss than people who did not use the machine.

Yet, these results could be challenged. For example, people who did not lose weight, despite using the machine, may have felt especially ashamed. Consequently, they might have withdrawn from the study. The data, therefore, are not accurate, because they may not include people who utilized the machine but gained weight. How can you ensure your study is conducted properly and is not liable to criticism?

Recruit participants

Research discoveries

People can more readily convince someone to undertake some behaviour—such as recycle their rubbish or complete a questionnaire—if they concede this act is inconvenient (Werner *et al.* 2002).

> People are more willing to complete a task that assists the community, but is otherwise monotonous, when they feel calm and content (Baumann & Kuhl 2005).
>
> When individuals perceive a task as a challenge, instead of a threat, they are not as likely to feel overwhelmed (Tomaka, Blascovich, Kelsey & Leitten 1993).

When people undertake research, they often need to ask other people — friends, acquaintances, colleagues, or strangers — to participate. This activity can be protracted as well as daunting.

Procedure 1	Example
In some studies, researchers recruit a random and diverse sample of people. In other studies, researchers recruit only the people who they feel may be especially informative and insightful, called purposive sampling. If the data are primarily quantitative—that is, numbers instead of words—you should recruit a random and diverse sample of people. If the data are primarily qualitative, you should recruit the most informed and insightful people.	Fred was not sure whether or not to recruit a random sample, because his research was designed to generate both quantitative and qualitative data. Eventually, he decided to recruit a random sample of participants from the TAFE, partly because he could not determine which people would be most informed about his topic.

Procedure 2	Example
Determine the number of people you would like to recruit. Roughly, if the data is quantitative, simple studies tend to examine about 50 people, whereas complex studies examine between 100 and 300 people. If the data is qualitative, researchers may interview about 10 people, conduct 3 to 5 focus groups, or both.	In his study, Fred and Barney together decided to interview 60 people, because the data were partly quantitative. Furthermore, the interviews were quite short; 60 people divided across two interviewers was thus feasible.

Procedure 3	Example
A variety of methods can be used to recruit participants. If the questions are delivered by email, text, or mail, researchers tend to use a database, such as all the employees in a specific company or all the members of a specific online forum. The researchers, obviously, will need permission from a suitable person before they can access this database. If the questions are delivered in person, researchers will often approach individuals on campuses, in shopping malls, or during some function. Always approach people in a peaceful rather than stressful setting. Emphasize that participating may be inconvenient but the study is important. Finally, if you feel daunted, perceive this task as a challenge—as an opportunity to learn from difficult experiences.	Fred decided to approach people in the grounds of his TAFE. He did not want to alarm anyone, so he did not approach anyone who was alone. To introduce himself, he said 'Hi, I'm Fred. I'm undertaking a study on attitudes at work. I know it's inconvenient, but I'd really appreciate if you could participate in this research. I think the results could be quite interesting.'

Procedure 4	Example
Collect any information you can about the people who refuse to participate. Later, you will be able to determine whether or not the people who participated were similar in profile to the people who did not participate. If they are not similar, the sample of participants might not reflect the broader population.	Fred and Barney estimated the age and recorded the sex of people who refused to participate in their study.

Introductory questions or comments

Research discoveries

While participants feel calm, their responses tend to be more accurate, diverse, and creative. In contrast, while participants feel sad, they tend to devote more effort into their answers (Hirt, Devers & McCrea 2008).

After people reflect upon their key values or achievements, they become less defensive. They will, therefore, answer subsequent questions more honestly (see Sherman & Cohen 2006).

While experiencing one emotion or state, people cannot accurately predict their attitudes or inclinations while experiencing another emotion or state, called the empathy gap (e.g. Nordgren, van der Pligt & van Harreveld 2006). For example, while content, people cannot predict their needs and preferences during stressful situations.

When researchers conduct interviews, focus groups or surveys, they first need to encourage the participants to respond honestly and devote effort to this task. That is, researchers must evoke the mindset or emotions that have been shown to foster sincerity, insight, and motivation.

Procedure 1	Example
To encourage people to participate in your study, you should summarize some of the concepts that you plan to examine. These summaries provide two benefits. First, the individuals will be sufficiently informed about the study to ensure they can decide whether or not they would like to participate. Indeed, ethics boards usually stipulate that researchers must outline the research and specify the rights of participants, called an explanatory statement. Second, if individuals are exposed to the main concepts from the outset, these topics will seem more familiar later. This sense of	Fred and Barney outlined their study to participants. They mentioned the study will explore a range of topics, specifically the relationships between inequality in income, emotions, trust, motivations at work, and the characteristics of organizations.

Procedure 1	Example
familiarity has been shown to increase the motivation of participants.	

Procedure 2	Example
Questions about demographics, such as the age of employees, should be deferred until the end. Instead, interviews, focus groups, or surveys should begin with questions about the strengths, achievements, or values of participants. That is, the first couple of questions should enable participants to highlight some of their desirable features.	The first question that Fred and Barney asked participants was 'What is your main motivation or value at work? Can you describe why this motivation or value is important to you?' This question is relevant to the research but, more importantly, enables participants to express their values and priorities.

Procedure 3	Example
Researchers sometimes precede some questions with a short introduction or justification. If the researchers want participants to express a diversity of novel and original ideas, these introductions should be facetious or uplifting. If the researchers want participants to think carefully, such as recall events that unfolded many years ago, these introductions should emphasize sad or poignant matters.	Before asking participants to indicate how they would feel if income differed more appreciably between employees and managers, Fred decided to include a facetious or uplifting introduction. That is, he knew that positive emotions tend to elicit more diverse and original answers.
	So, he told participants about an employee who was accused unfairly of an offence. The managers had dismissed the protestations of this employee. Eventually, the actual perpetrator was discovered. Although contrived, Fred knew this tale would soon be true.
	Before delivering the questions designed to generate quantitative data, however, Fred decided to include more sobering introduction.

Procedure 3	Example
	He knew that feelings of sadness often inspire contemplation. Therefore, before presenting these questions, he mentioned that 'The rate of mental illness and injustice has increased dramatically in Australia over the last three decades. These questions revolve around some of these issues'.

Procedure 4	Example
Some questions relate to the feelings, attitudes, or behaviours of people in specific contexts or states, such as 'How do you feel when your role is unclear?' Before answering these questions, participants should be encouraged to imagine themselves in this context or state as vividly as possible.	Fred wanted to determine how participants would feel if they knew their colleagues were more driven to excel than to help one another. To ensure that participants imagine this possibility as vividly as possibly, Fred decided to first ask these individuals to specify the person they know who is most selfish instead of supportive. He then decided to ask these individuals to imagine this person is waiting outside and will soon evaluate their performance. Finally, Fred planned to ask participants how they would feel in response to this scenario.

Recall all details

During interviews and focus groups, researchers will usually record, but will sometimes transcribe, the answers of participants. Unfortunately, researchers sometimes forget to transcribe other details that seem peripheral but could actually influence the results, such as the temperature and lighting in the room, the ambient noise, the mood of participants, and other incidental remarks or events.

Research discoveries

On sunny days, compared to rainy days, people are more likely to value qualities that are beneficial during pleasant climates, such as social skills. On rainy days, people are more likely to value intelligence and reflection (Simonsohn 2007).

The time of day also affects the attitudes and preferences of people. Before lunch or dinner, people tend to be hungry. Hunger shapes the opinions of individuals. To demonstrate with an amusing example, while they are hungry, males tend to prefer heavier women than lighter women. They are also more likely to be dissatisfied with their salary (Nelson & Morrison 2005).

The mood of people also affects their responses. When people feel proud, they value products that relate to status, such as an expensive watch. When people feel content, however, they value products that relate to their home, such as a bed (Griskevicius, Shiota & Nowlis 2010).

Procedure 1	Example
If the questions are delivered in person, the researcher should record details such as whether the surroundings are hot or cold, whether the room is light or dim, whether the participants seem excited or bored, as well as other events, such as noises.	Fred constructed an inventory that is designed to orient his attention to all the details that could be relevant. The inventory included: ▪ Temperature… ▪ Lighting… ▪ Noise… ▪ Mood… ▪ Pictures… ▪ Remarks of participants before the questions were posed… ▪ Remarks of participants after the questions had been answered…

Ethical and supportive behaviour

To conform to the ethical principles and guidelines of research, the researchers need to treat participants with respect and dignity. They need to ensure the participants feel as comfortable as possible.

Research discoveries

When the environment or surroundings are light blue or green, people feel both more composed and more patient (e.g. Gorn *et al.* 2004).

Procedure 1	Example
Most institutions have formed an ethics committee. This committee assesses whether or not research projects are ethical and suitable. You must comply with the principles and guidelines that are imposed by this committee. In general, these committees dictate that researchers must ensure that: • Potential participants understand all the risks and discomfort of a study before they agree to participate. • Potential participants do not feel any obligation to participate. For example, if the researcher knows the manager of someone, this person may feel compelled to participate. Such obligation, called implicit coercion, should be avoided. • Participants are able to withdraw from the study at any time. • Participants are not deceived during the study • The responses of participants are anonymous • The data are stored in a secure place for several years and then destroyed • Participants do not experience more unpleasant emotions than they would on a typical day. Occasionally, but infrequently, ethics committees will permit researchers to breach these principles, but only if the benefits of these violations significantly outweigh the drawbacks.	Fred and Barney were instructed to complete an ethics application—a questionnaire in which they are asked to answer various questions about their research. The ethics committee acknowledged the procedures that Fred and Barney had formulated were ethical.

Chapter 7

Analysing the data you collected

On December 31, 2009, *A Current Affair* presented the predictions of two psychics. These two psychics forecasted several events that may unfold during 2010. The psychics predicted that Susan Boyle will retire, the Queen and Elton John will be gravely ill, Barack Obama will be the victim of an attempted assassination, and Tony Abbott will not contest the election, none of which materialized.

They did, admittedly, predict the weather will be erratic and petrol prices will rise. These prophecies, however, do not necessarily indicate these individuals are psychic. Many people, obviously, could have predicted these possibilities.

To assess psychic powers, we need some statistic that accurately reflects whether psychics outperform other people on these predictions. That is, we need some technique to compare groups, in this instance psychic people and other people, on various measures. Which techniques should we apply to assess our hypotheses?

Examine correlations

Research discoveries

If people feel uncertain or unsure about something, they are more likely to detect patterns or relationships in events that are actually random or unrelated to each other (Proulx & Heine 2006). Therefore, researchers need to apply rigorous methods, rather than depend on their own perceptions, to analyse data.

Hundreds of software packages, and thousands of techniques, have been developed to analyse quantitative data. Rather than describe all these packages and techniques in this book, this chapter will illustrate a few key techniques. These techniques are sufficient for many research projects and also demonstrate a few key principles.

Often, researchers merely need to examine whether or not two variables, such as inequality in income and anxiety are related to each other. A statistic, called the Pearson product moment correlation—or simply a correlation—resolves this question.

Procedure 1	Example
Insert the data into an Excel sheet. Each column should correspond to one variable, such as income inequality. Each row should correspond to one participant.	Fred inserted the data into a spreadsheet. Some of the responses on income inequality and anxiety appear in the following extract of the data.
	In this example, from this limited sample of data, a pattern seems to emerge. The high levels of inequality seem to coincide with the higher levels of anxiety. The lower levels of inequality seem to coincide with the low levels of anxiety. That is, income inequality seems to be positively related to anxiety.

Income inequality	Anxiety
0.97	9
0.45	5
0.96	9
0.15	2
0.56	6
0.07	1
0.85	6

Procedure 2	Example
Rather than merely scan the data, researchers must calculate an objective measure to determine whether or not two variables are	Fred followed these steps. This procedure generated the number .47. Thus, the correlation is .47.

Procedure 2	Example
related. To calculate this measure, called a correlation: • Place the cursor in an empty cell. • Select the Formulas tab at the top of Excel. • Then select the options 'More functions' and 'Statistical'. Scroll down the list of options until you can uncover and choose CORREL. • In the box labelled Array 1, type the cell numbers that correspond to the first and last data point of the first column. Separate these cells by a colon, such as A2: A52 • In the box labelled Array 2, type the cell numbers that correspond to the first and last data point of the second column, such as B2: B52. • Then press OK.	Fred knew that Barney would be too lethargic to calculate this correlation himself. Indeed, Fred even hoped that Barney would not calculate this correlation. His plan depended on this tendency of Barney to copy Fred.

Procedure 3	Example
You then need to interpret this correlation. This number can vary from -1 to +1. A positive number indicates the two variables are positively associated with each other. A negative number indicates the two variables are negatively associated with each other. A 0 indicates the two variables are not related to each other.	The correlation that Fred generated was greater than zero. This finding, therefore, indicates that inequality in income is positively related to anxiety. That is, as inequality in income escalates, the level of anxiety is likely to increase as well. If the correlation had been negative, Fred would have concluded that income inequality is negatively related to anxiety. That is, as inequality in income increases, the level of anxiety is likely to decrease.

Procedure 4	Example
Before celebrating, however, one complication needs to be considered. The correlation you calculated was derived from only a sample of participants at a particular time and, therefore, is called the sample correlation. This value might differ slightly from the true correlation—the correlation that would be calculated if you examined all participants at all times, called the population correlation.	Fred undertook these four steps to calculate the p value. For the first step, he typed the formula:
	$= (1 + .47) / (1 - .47)$
	which equals about 2.774. For the second step, he typed the formula:
	$= .5 * LOG(2.774, 2.7182)$
	which equals about .5102. Actually, the formula did not work initially. But then he removed the spaces, and the formula worked. For the third step, he typed the formula:
If the sample correlation is very high, such as .95, you can be quite sure the population or true correlation would be positive a well. If the sample correlation is very low, such as -.95, you can be quite sure the population of true correlation would be negative as well. But if your correlation is close to zero, such as .12, you cannot be certain whether or not the population or true correlation would be positive or negative.	$= 1 / sqrt(60)$
	which equals about .129. For the final step, he typed the formula:
	$= (1 - Normdist(.5102, 0, .129, TRUE)) * 2$
	which equals about .000077 Because the final answer, the p value, is less than .05, Fred can be 95% certain his correlation is sufficiently different from 0. Admittedly, the true correlation might not equal his sample correlation of .47. Nevertheless, because his sample correlation is significantly greater than 0, he can be quite certain the true correlation must be positive as well. In short, he can confident that inequality in income really is positively associated with anxiety.
So, how can you determine whether your sample correlation is high enough to conclude the true correlation is positive? Likewise, how can you determine if your sample correlation is low enough to conclude the true correlation is negative? A technique has been developed to answer this question. You merely need to follow a series of steps, each of which are simple but might seem complex at first. These steps are even simpler if you can access a statistical software package, such as SPSS.	If the p value had been greater than .05, he could not be certain the true correlation is also greater than zero. He could not conclude confidently that inequality in income is positively associated with anxiety.

Procedure 4	Example
First, in any cell in Excel, type the formula: $= (1 + r) / (1 - r)$ However, replace the letter r with your correlation. Second, to calculate an index called z, in any cell, type the formula: $= .5 * LOG(first answer, 2.7182)$ However, replace the label first answer with your answer to the first formula. Third, to calculate an index called se, in any cell, type the formula: $= 1 / sqrt(n)$ However, replace the n with the number of participants who answered these questions. Finally, to calculate an index called the p value, in any cell, type the formula: $= (1 - Normdist(z, 0, se, TRUE)) * 2$ However, rather than z or se, include the z index and se value you calculated using the previous two formulas. If this p value that emerges is less than .05, you can be 95% certain your correlation is sufficiently different from 0.	

Compare groups with t tests and chi-square tests of independence

Research discoveries

When individuals perceive themselves as part of a cohesive group or community, they are sometimes more likely to overlook differences between specific people. Their conclusions about whether or not two groups differ on some variable, such as anxiety, may be misguided (Stapel & Van der Zee 2006). Rigorous statistical tests are needed to prevent these problems.

Interestingly, this discovery was reported by Dietrich Stapel, a researcher who has since been accused of fraud. This discovery, therefore, should be regarded as tentative.

Sometimes, you may want to compare two groups on some variable. You may, for example, want to compare males and females on anxiety. Similarly, if you undertook an experiment, you may want to compare the two conditions on some outcome. A technique called an independent samples t test, or merely a t test, can fulfil this purpose.

Procedure 1	Example
Insert the data on one question or measure into an Excel sheet. For this example, construct two columns, each associated with one group or condition.	Fred inserted the data into an Excel sheet. The first column represented the anxiety levels of male participants. The second column represented the anxiety levels of female participants.

Procedure 2	Example
To conduct this t test: ▪ Place the cursor in an empty cell. ▪ Select the Formulas tab at the top of Excel. ▪ Then select the options 'More	Fred followed these steps. This procedure generated the number .032.

Procedure 2	Example
functions' and 'Statistical'. Scroll down the list of options until you can uncover and choose T.TEST. • In the box labelled Array 1, type the cell numbers that correspond to the first and last data point of the first column. Separate these cells by a colon, such as A2: A52 • In the box labelled Array 2, type the cell numbers that correspond to the first and last data point of the second column, such as B2: B52. • In the box labelled tails, enter 2 • Similarly, in a the box labelled type, also enter 3 • Then press OK.	

Procedure 3	Example
You now need to interpret this number. If this number, which is also called a p value, is less than .05, you can be 95% certain these groups differ significantly from each other on this variable. That is, even if you collected data from all participants at all times, you would be very confident the groups would still differ on this variable.	Because Fred uncovered a p value that is less than .05 he could be 95% sure that males and females really differ on anxiety. Although unfeasible, if he had collected data from all males and females at all times, he would probably still discover the sexes differ from each other on anxiety.

Procedure 4	Example
Finally, especially if the groups differed from each other, you need to establish which group generated the higher scores. To achieve this goal, calculate the average score for each group. Specifically:	Fred followed these instructions. He discovered the average level of anxiety in males is 7.4. He discovered the average level of anxiety in females is 6.8. He, therefore, concluded that males

Procedure 4	Example
<ul><li>Under the first column, type =AVERAGE(A2: A50)</li><li>However, rather than A2 and A50, write the cell numbers that correspond to the first and last number in this column.</li><li>Under the second column, type =AVERAGE(B2: B50)</li><li>But again, rather than B2 and B50, write the cell numbers that correspond to the first and last number in this column.</li><li>Determine which average is higher.</li></ul>	were significantly more anxious than females.

Procedure 5	Example
Undertake another t-test to compare the people who agreed to participate to the people who refused to participate on age or other numerical variables that you could estimate.	Fred was able to estimate the age of both the people who agreed to participate and the people who refused to participate. He conducted a t-test to ascertain whether age, as estimated by the researchers, differed between these groups. In this instance, the p value exceeded .05. Consequently, Fred could not confidently conclude that people who participated differed from people who refused to participate on age. If the p values had been less than .05, Fred would have been 95% certain that people who agreed to participated differed from people who refused to participate on age. His sample of participants, therefore, would have diverged from the broader population. The results of his study would not apply

Procedure 5	Example
	to people in general. Fred would have needed to concede this limitation in his report.

Age, level of anxiety, and height are called numerical variables. That is, each person is assigned a number on these variables, such as 38, 5, or 172. The t-test is used to compare groups on numerical variables, such as age.

The sex and hair colour of people, in contrast, are called categorical variables; each person is assigned a category on these variables, such as female or brown. A procedure called a chi-square test of independence is used to compare groups on categorical variables.

Procedure 1	Example
A chi-square test of independence compares groups, e.g. people who agreed to participate and people who refused to participate, on a categorical variable, such as sex. To conduct this test, you need to follow several laborious but simple steps. For each group or condition, count the frequency of every category, such as the number of males and number of females. Tabulate this information. Each row should represent one group, and each column one category.	Of the males who Fred and Barney were approached, 20 agreed to participate and 45 refused to participate. Of the females who Fred and Barney approached, 40 agreed to participate and 30 refused to participate. Fred constructed the following table to display this information: <table><tr><td></td><td>Males</td><td>Females</td></tr><tr><td>Agreed</td><td>20</td><td>40</td></tr><tr><td>Refused</td><td>45</td><td>30</td></tr></table>

Procedure 2	Example
Calculate the sum of each column and each row. Also calculate the total number of people.	Fred calculated the sum of each column and row as well as the total number of people. <table><tr><td></td><td>Males</td><td>Females</td><td>Totals</td></tr><tr><td>Agreed</td><td>20</td><td>40</td><td>60</td></tr><tr><td>Refused</td><td>45</td><td>30</td><td>75</td></tr><tr><td>Totals</td><td>65</td><td>70</td><td>135</td></tr></table>

Procedure 3	Example
Using these numbers, construct another table in which each cell equals: • the sum of that column x the sum of that row/ the total number of people.	Fred followed this advice. In the cell that corresponds to males who agreed to participate, for example, the formula equals the sum of that column, 65, multiplied by the sum of that row, 60, divided by the total, 135. Fred applied the same procedure to the other three cells:

	Males	Females	Totals
Agreed	65 x 60 / 135	70 x 60 / 135	60
Refused	65 x 75/ 135	70 x 75 / 135	75
Totals	65	70	135

Fred then completed the arithmetic to generate the final table:

	Males	Females	Totals
Agreed	29	31	60
Refused	36	39	75
Totals	65	70	135

This table is called the expected frequencies. In essence, these numbers reflect the frequencies that Fred would expect if the ratio of males and females was the same in both groups—that is, the people who agreed to participate and the people who refused to participate.

Procedure 4	Example
Compute a statistical called the chi-square. To compute this statistic: • For all the cells, calculate the difference between the expected frequency, as calculated in the	Fred followed this procedure. For each cell, he computed the difference between the expected and actual frequency.

	Males	Females
Agreed	20-29 = -9	40-31 = -9
Refused	45-36 = -9	30-39 = -9

Procedure 4	Example
previous step, and the actual frequency • Square this difference • Divide the answer by the expected frequency • Sum all the answers.	Second, he squared these differences: 		Males	Females
---	---	---
Agreed	81	81
Refused	81	81 | Third, he divided these squared differences by the expected frequency: |	Males	Females
---	---	---
Agreed	81 / 29 = 2.8	81 / 31 = 2.6
Refused	81 / 36 = 2.3	81 / 39 = 2.1	 Finally, he summed these four answers and generated the number 9.7. The chi square value was thus 9.7.

Procedure 5	Example
A chi square value, such as 9.7, is initially meaningless. To interpret this value, you need to translate the chi square statistic into a p value. To achieve this goal, in an empty cell in Excel, enter: • =CHISQ.DIST.RT(9.7,1) However: • Instead of 9.7 include the chi square value that you calculated • Replace this 1 with (number of rows – 1) x (the number of columns – 1).	In this example, the number of rows and the number of columns were both 2. So (number of rows – 1) x (the number of columns – 1) equals (2 – 1) x (2 - 1), which equals 1 x 1 or just 1. Fred, therefore, entered =CHISQ.DIST.RT(9.7,1) into Excel and generated the answer .002.

Procedure 6	Example
You now need to interpret this p value. If this p value is less than .05, you can be 95% certain these	Because Fred uncovered a p value that is less than .05 he could be 95% sure that people who agreed

Procedure 6	Example
groups differ significantly from each other on this variable. That is, even if you collected data from all participants at all times, you would be very confident the groups would still differ from each other on this variable.	to participate and people who refused to participate differed on sex. The proportion of females was higher in the people who agreed to participate than in the people who refused to participate. This difference needs to be conceded in his report.

Excel offers many other functions. For example, one statistical function, FREQUENCY, can be used to count the number of times that participants specified a particular response.

Nevertheless, if you want to undertake more complex analyses, you should access or purchase specialized software, such as SPSS or MPLUS. These statistical packages enable researchers to examine more variables at the same time. In addition, these statistical packages enables researchers to estimate whether two variables would have been related—or two groups would have differed from each other—had everyone been average on another variable.

Qualitative techniques: Thematic analysis

A variety of approaches can be utilized to analyse qualitative data, including the responses of participants during interviews or focus groups. Some researchers attempt to extract themes or patterns from reading the responses. Other researchers utilize more systematic procedures.

Research discoveries

Some researchers utilize a package called the Linguistic Inquiry and Word Count program. This program counts the number of times participants utilized various sets of words, such as positive words or negative words.

By analysing the frequency with which they use various words, researchers can gain significant insight into the personality or inclinations of people (Pennebaker & King 1999). For example, people who seldom use the words I, me, or my have frequently been shown to embrace novel perspectives and opportunities. People who often refer to positive emotions tend to be extraverted, agreeable, and stable. People who often use the words but, without, or except tend to be introverted. People who often refer to terms like since or because tend to be anxious.

Experts can also derive other insights from a close examination of words. To illustrate, if people refer to tangible features, like 'the manager shed tears', they most likely feel the person they have described does not often demonstrate this behaviour. If people refer to intangible qualities, like 'the manager was upset', they most likely feel the person they have described often demonstrates this behaviour (Maass, Ceccarelli & Rudin 1996), called a linguistic bias.

One effective technique to analyse qualitative data is called thematic analysis (Braun & Clarke 2006), an approach that is applicable in many circumstances. In essence, researchers assign codes to specific answers or sentences. Next, they uncover clusters of related codes to form themes. Finally, these themes are refined, compared, and integrated to form a cohesive account of the data.

Procedure 1	Example
Initially, skim all the qualitative data that you have collected on a topic. Then read the data a couple of times in depth. While skimming or reading the data, record any ideas or impressions that emerge.	Fred skimmed, and then read, the responses he had collected during the interviews. In particular, he collected responses to three questions: ▪ How would you feel if income differed more appreciably between employees and managers? ▪ How you would you feel if you knew that your colleagues were more driven to succeed than to help one another? ▪ How would you feel if you did not trust your colleagues? Some typical responses included: ▪ 'Initially, when I found out that incomes vary a lot across individuals, I was excited. I thought I could be one of those people that could earn a lot of money. But, then I wondered whether people would be jealous and suspicious of one

Procedure 1	Example
	another' • 'If I thought everyone was just driven to succeed, I'd try to be helpful to my colleagues. I'd figure that nobody else would be so helpful, and so I'd be valued'.

Procedure 2	Example
Assign each segment of data—perhaps each distinct thought or sentence—a code. Codes are usually a few words that summarize these segments of data.	Fred assigned codes to all the qualitative data. He extracted about 40 different codes. For example: • He formulated the code 'Increasing concern over inequality over time' to represent the remark 'Initially, when I found out that incomes vary a lot across individuals, I was excited. I thought I could be one of those people that could earn a lot of money. But, then I wondered whether people would be jealous and suspicious of one another' • He formulated the code 'Being cooperative is a niche' to represent the remark 'If I thought everyone was just driven to succeed, I'd try to be helpful to my colleagues. I'd figure that nobody else would be so helpful, and so I'd be valued'. • He also uncovered other codes, such as 'Develop a unique skill', to represent other responses.

Procedure 3	Example
Compare and integrate codes to uncover meaningful themes and insights. Write a paragraph or so to define each theme.	Fred felt that two of his codes— 'Being cooperative is a niche' and 'Develop a unique skill'—seemed to be related to each other. Specifically, as these codes imply, in competitive settings, some employees like to cultivate a distinct role. If they develop a distinct role, they feel somewhat protected from the competitive orientation of colleagues. He called this theme 'Cultivate a distinct role'. In addition, Fred uncovered eight other themes as well.

Fred constructed a paragraph to define 'Cultivate a distinct role'. He wrote 'In competitive settings, employees attempt to highlight their distinct capabilities, contributions, and activities. They attempt to differentiate themselves from their colleagues and, therefore, may behave cooperatively in a competitive environment'. |

Procedure 4	Example
Reread the responses of participants to ensure all the data conform to these themes. If necessary, refine your definition of these themes to ensure they explain all the data.	Fred discovered that one of the themes—'Cultivate a distinct role'—corresponds to many of the responses. Nevertheless, after rereading the data and his codes, Fred felt this theme comprised a broader array of roles that he initially realized. So, when he redefined this theme, he attempted to summarize this diversity of roles. Specifically, he added 'Employees may attempt to depict themselves as the person who offers

Procedure 4	Example
	encouragement, fixes equipment, challenges management, or suggests creative possibilities, for instance'.

Procedure 5	Example
Finally, reflect upon how these themes are related to one another. You could classify the themes into several clusters. You could arrange the themes in some order.	Fred realized that his themes could be arranged in order, from the practices that employees initially implement to the practices that employees implement after significant experience in the workplace.

Chapter 8

Interpreting the data

On 24 October 2011, *A Current Affair* reported a story on the cost of housing and supporting asylum seekers. According to this report, over the last financial year, detention centres in Australia cost taxpayers over $800 million. Some these expenses were needed to buy plasma TVs and to operate internet cafés.

The report highlighted that costs are escalating. For example, costs have almost doubled since the previous year.

Yet, this conclusion may be misleading. This rise in costs one year might not indicate that expenses are escalating over time. Instead, expenses may have been anomalously, and perhaps unreasonably, low the year before. The rise in expenses this year may not reflect an overarching trend. Instead, this rise may reflect the resumption of usual costs. Alternatively, this rise may reflect the attempt of authorities to compensate and offset previous neglect. The resumption to usual levels is called regression to the mean.

Students often extract misleading or premature conclusions from their data. How can you avoid these errors?

Consider response biases

The responses of participants to questions are often inaccurate. For example, suppose people are asked, on a scale of 1 to 10, the extent to which they agree with the statement 'I should wear a helmet when I ride a bicycle'. Many biases may shape their responses to this question.

First, some people demonstrate a bias called social desirability bias, in which they inflate their strengths and trivialize their limitations. These individuals may assume they always follow the law and, therefore, strongly agree with this statement. Second, some people tend to agree with most statements, almost regardless of the content, called an acquiescence bias. Third, some people underestimate their susceptibility to hazards, called the optimism bias. These individuals may presume they are not prone to accidents and, therefore, will tend to disagree with this statement.

Research discoveries

People who are especially motivated to pursue their personal aspirations are often unaware of their limitations. People who are especially motivated to fulfil their duties or obligations often conceal their doubts and uncertainties about themselves (Leonardelli, Lakin & Arkin 2007).

People who are not especially educated or intelligent—but are somewhat conscientious or prejudiced—often demonstrate the acquiescence bias. If asked to specify the extent to which they agree or disagree with statements, they tend to agree (Meisenberg & Williams 2008).

After people contemplate their personal values, they do not feel as fragile. As this fragility diminishes, they become less susceptible to the optimism bias and recognize they are as vulnerable to hazards as everyone else (Sherman *et al.* 2009).

All these biases, and many other tendencies as well, can distort the results. Specifically, these biases are spurious variables and inflate the relationship between two variables.

To illustrate, suppose the researcher wants to examine whether inequality in income is related to anxiety. In this study, participants are asked to indicate the extent to which they agree with two statements on a scale of 1 to 10: 'At this organizations, the incomes of employees vary considerably' and 'At this organization, many people feel anxious'.

Now suppose that half or so of the participants demonstrate the acquiescence bias and, therefore, strongly agree with these two statements. Because of this acquiescence bias, the people who feel that incomes vary considerably across the organization are also the people who feel that many people are anxious. The researcher will, therefore, conclude that income inequality is associated with anxiety, even if these variables do not actually affect each other.

Procedure 1	Example
Identify questions in your study that, to some extent, measure the extent to which people perceive themselves as capable, cooperative, or moral. These questions are susceptible to social desirability biases. Any correlations between these variables could be misleading.	Fred scanned all the questions he asked participants. He realized that he did not ask individuals about their own capabilities or behaviours. Instead, he asked individuals to express their opinions or perceptions of their work environment and work colleagues. Consequently, he concluded that none of his questions were especially sensitive to social desirability biases.

Procedure 2	Example
Identify questions in your study in which participants indicate the degree to which they agree or disagree with some statement. These questions are susceptible to the acquiescence bias. Again, any correlations between these variables could be misleading.	Fred realized that he had asked participants to specify the extent to which they agree or disagree that 'Incomes vary considerably across the organization' and 'Employees tend to distrust one another'. He therefore conceded that a correlation between these questions could be misleading. That is, because of the acquiescence bias, a subset of participants may have expressed strong agreement to these questions, inflating the relationship between these variables.

Procedure 3	Example
Identify questions in your study in which participants need to estimate their susceptibility to some hazard or threat. These questions are particularly	As Fred realized, in his study, participants did not need to estimate their susceptibility to hazards or threats. The optimism bias, therefore, is unlikely to contaminate the results of his study.

Procedure 3	Example
susceptible to the optimism bias. Again, any correlations between these variables could be misleading.	Yet, Fred knew that Barney may be vulnerable to this bias. He assumed that Barney did not realize that he was susceptible to a plot that could expose his treachery—a plot that was underway.

Consider personal biases

Research discoveries

People tend to underestimate their susceptibility to various biases. That is, they assume that other individuals are more vulnerable to biases than are they (Pronin, Lin & Ross 2002). For example, individuals presume they are not as likely as the average person to be swayed by advertisements (Paul, Salwen & Dupagne 2000).

People tend to assume that conspicuous or common events are related to each other, sometimes called illusory correlations (e.g. Johnson, Mullen, Carlson & Southwick 2001). To illustrate, suppose that most of the customers in a retail store are young rather than old. In addition, suppose that most of the customers are rude instead of friendly. In this instance, the customers tend to be young as well as rude. Consequently, people will tend to assume, and perhaps incorrectly, that young people are rude.

Like participants, researchers are also prone to various biases. That is, their conclusions are sometimes misguided. Qualitative data are especially susceptible to these biases.

Procedure 1	Example
If the data are qualitative, conclusions may represent illusory correlations. That is, if two concepts were often mentioned, you may have assumed incorrectly these concepts are indeed related to each other. Refer to specific evidence to justify any claims that two variables are related to each other.	During the interviews that Fred and Barney conducted, many participants felt they would be especially motivated to excel rather than cooperate with colleagues. In addition, participants conceded they would feel anxious if they did not trust colleagues. Fred concluded, therefore, that motivation to excel should provoke

Procedure 1	Example
	anxiety.
	But then, Fred began to doubt this conclusion. Because motivation to excel and anxiety were both mentioned frequently, Fred may have incorrectly assumed these variables were related to each other.
	So, he decided to reread the responses of participants to determine whether or not people actually described the sequence of events that relate motivation to excel to anxiety. He discovered that four of the participants claimed to feel suspicious, vigilant, agitated, and anxious in workgroups in which their colleagues are very ambitious and motivated to excel. These claims seem to support the argument that a motivation to excel provokes anxiety in colleagues.

Consider unexpected data

Research discoveries

In noisy or stressful environments, individuals tend to reach decisions prematurely. Consequently, they might dismiss findings that contradict their predictions (Kruglanski & Webster 1991).

When people work near a visible light globe that is on, their insight improves (Slepian *et al.* 2010). For example, they can probably explain unexpected results more effectively.

When people attempt to uncover a specific and large number of possible solutions to a problem, such as 20 or 25, without evaluating or judging these possibilities, their ideas tend to be more creative (Litchfield 2009).

Some of the results may not align to your predictions or hypotheses. Often, researchers trivialize these unforeseen results. They might, for example, refer to these findings as anomalies or outliers.

Yet, when people try to explain these surprising findings, their thoughts are more likely to be original and useful, and their arguments insightful.

Procedure 1	Example
Identify data or findings, such as specific comments or correlations, that differed from your expectations. For each unforeseen result, first skim the summaries you have written about past research that may be relevant to this finding. Second, attempt to list 10 possible explanations. Include explanations that seem unusual or unlikely. Third, try to refine and integrate some of these explanations to form a more plausible account of these results.	Fred was surprised to discover that income inequality was positively associated with unjust procedures. That is, if incomes varied appreciably across employees and managers, the procedures were more likely to be perceived as unfair. Fred had not formed any hypotheses about whether or not these variables should be related to each other. So, this finding did not contradict his hypotheses but was not predicted either. Fred skimmed the summaries he had constructed about past research on justice and fairness. He then decided to list 10 or so possible explanations of this finding. Examples include: • When procedures are flawed, people who often lie may be able to inflate their contributions and, therefore, receive unwarranted promotions and bonuses. • When incomes are unequal, people just assume the procedures must be unfair to explain this variability in pay. • When incomes are unequal, people may not be able to concentrate as well. The procedures they construct might, therefore, be flawed. Fred then reflected upon whether

Procedure 1	Example
	or not some of these explanations can be integrated to form a more viable account. In the end, he decided that income inequality may reduce any faith in the procedures. Consequently, people are too cynical to devote effort into improving or refining these procedures. Injustices and shortcomings are never resolved.

Chapter 9

Planning the report

On 8 December 2007, *Today Tonight* reported a story about some of the unintended effects of Gardasil—the vaccine that diminishes the likelihood of cervical cancer. One girl for example, after receiving the drug, claimed to feel dizzy, nauseous, weak on the ride side of her body, and even prone to hallucinations. Another girl reported back pain and unpleasant sensations in her arms. Indeed, many people have reported adverse reactions.

However, these concerns about Gardasil may be gravely inflated. About one in every 4,400 women seems to experience adverse reactions. Conceivably, even if the injections did not contain Gardasil, many people may still experience these reactions. That is, when people anticipate an injection, the likelihood of various symptoms increases. Therefore, to assess whether Gardasil provokes these reactions, researchers need to compare people who had been injected with this chemical to people who had been injected with no active chemical, called a sham control.

So, to evaluate research, the reader needs to know the exact procedures that were administered to the control group. Without this information, the research is uninformative. How can you ensure you include all the relevant information in your report?

Planning the main sections of a report

Besides a title and appendix, most reports comprise six main sections:

- A summary or abstract to present the aims of this research and to outline the methods, results, and conclusions.

- An introduction to highlight the importance of this topic as well as to justify the predictions.

- A method section to describe the participants, the materials, and the procedures.

- A results section to summarize the data, including any statistical tests or qualitative analyses.

- A discussion section to describe the implications of these results.

- A reference section that lists all the sources that were cited in the report.

These sections are not usually written in the same order in which they appear. Instead, researchers tend to write the method, results, introduction, discussion, and summary in that order.

Research discoveries

To plan a report effectively, people need to be able to contemplate and transform many concepts in their mind at the same time. After they remember a time in which they were granted some power, influence, or authority, their capacity to complete this task improves (Smith, Jostmann, Galinsky & van Dijk 2008).

Procedure 1	Example
If possible, while you plan the report, imagine that you are an expert in this field and the report has been commissioned by some important person or organization. When individuals experience this feeling of influence, they tend to plan and to organize their ideas more effectively.	Fred imagined that he was now a renowned social scientist. He pretended, for a moment, that he had been asked by a government minister to prepare this report.

Procedure 2: The method section	Example
Construct bullet points that summarize the key features of your method. First, indicate the number	To summarize the method, Fred initially constructed the following bullet points:

Procedure 2: The method section	Example
and demographics of your participants as well as the procedures you applied to recruit these individuals. Second, describe the measures or materials that you constructed or utilized in this study. Finally, describe the procedures or activities that participants completed.	Participants: • 60 employees, 20 males and 40 females, were recruited • The age of participants ranged from 30 to 50 • All participants had been employed in their current workplace for more than six months • Participants were recruited from the grounds of a TAFE. Materials and procedure: • The questionnaire included measures of income inequality, anxiety, trust, motivations at work, fairness of procedures, and workplace culture. • The questions to assess motivation at work and fairness of procedures were derived from established scales; describe these scales • Include sample questions. Procedure: • Participants were interviewed individually. • They were informed the study is designed to examine the relationships between income equality, workplace culture, and employee motivation and emotion. • They first completed the questionnaire. • Next, a structured interview was conducted in which participants discussed the implications of income inequality, motivations to excel, and distrust.

Procedure 3: The results section	Example
Construct bullet points that summarize the key features of your results. For example, present the correlation between various pairs of variables. In addition, if you want to compare specific conditions on some variable, present the average score of each group as well as the results of t tests, chi square tests of independence, or other techniques. Furthermore, if the data is qualitative, you may define the main themes that emerged and include quotes to illustrate these themes.	To summarize the results, Fred initially constructed the following bullet points. Correlations included: • Income inequality and anxiety, $r = .47$ • Income inequality and motivation to excel, $r = .54$ • Income inequality and trust, $r = .38$ • Motivation to excel and trust, $r = .10$ • Trust and anxiety, $r = .45$ • Most of these correlations significantly differed from 0; $p > .05$ in each instance • However, the correlation between the motivation to excel and trust was not significant. Some tests were conducted to compare people who agreed to participate with the people who did not agree to participate. These tests showed that: • Age did not differ between people who agreed to participate and people who did not agree to participate • Males, however, were more inclined than females to refuse the request to participate. • This sample, therefore, may not be representative of the broader population but may be skewed towards females. Finally, Fred summarized the themes that emerged, coupled with some sample quotes, such as: • Cultivate a distinct role (e.g. 'If I

Procedure 2: The method section	Example
	thought everyone was just driven to succeed, I'd try to be helpful to my colleagues. I'd figure that nobody else would be so helpful, and so I'd be valued'). ■ Excitement over possibilities (e.g. 'I thought that if some people can make it, then I can make it as well').

Procedure 4: The introduction	Example
Construct bullet points that summarize the key features of your introduction. Your introduction begins with paragraphs that justify the significance of your topic and ends with the aims or hypotheses of your study. The remainder of your introduction is primarily a cohesive series of arguments, explanations, and theories that justify your aim and hypotheses. In addition, past research that supports these arguments, explanations, and theories are included.	To write the introduction, Fred constructed a series of bullet points. First, he planned the paragraphs that justified the significance of this topic. Specifically, he wanted to include striking statistics about income inequality or anxiety as well as highlight the controversies about this topic: ■ Last year, a young woman complained to her friends that her workplace was competitive and brutal two days before committing suicide. ■ Anxiety, depression, suicide, crime, teenage pregnancy and many other problems seem rife today in Western nations, such as the US and Australia, and may be increasing. ■ Some research indicates that inequality in income—which has also increased in these nations— is the primary cause of all these problems ■ Yet two limitations in the literature have not been resolved.

Procedure 4: The introduction	Example
	▪ First, researchers have not clarified why income inequality causes these problems.
	▪ Indeed, some people even claim that observed associations between income inequality and other problems are overestimated and can be ascribed to spurious variables
	▪ Second, research has not established whether inequality within organizations, rather than inequality within nations, also provokes anxiety and other problems.
	Fred then summarized the arguments he could invoke to justify his hypotheses:
	▪ Income inequality highlights the benefits of competition instead of cooperation.
	▪ When incomes are unequal, people are, therefore, especially motivated to compete.
	▪ They also assume that other people are motivated to compete, curbing trust.
	▪ Furthermore, if motivated to compete, cooperation declines, and so this decrease in trust is perceptive.
	▪ Nevertheless, as trust declines, people become vigilant.
	▪ They also feel that nobody will help them if problems unfold, called an insecure attachment.
	▪ So, moments of anxiety tend to persist.
	▪ These problems are especially pronounced in roles in which

Procedure 4: The introduction	Example
	employees do depend on one another.
	Fred then collected research that supports each contention and also summarized the aim and hypotheses of this study.

Procedure 5: The discussion	Example
Construct bullet points that summarize the key features of your discussion. In particular, this section should include a paragraph or two that briefly outlines the aim, method, and results. Next, the discussion presents an explanation, and specifies the implications, of each important result. Finally, the discussion concludes with the limitations of this study, potential improvements that could be included in the future, as well as the practical benefits of this study.	Fred constructed a series of bullet points to plan the discussion. Specifically, he initially wrote: • This study examined whether income inequality within organizations evokes anxiety as well as whether motivation to excel and distrust mediate this relationship. • In general, the results support the hypotheses. He then decided to present the explanations and specify the implications of each key finding, sometimes referring to the qualitative data as well, such as: • The finding that income inequality correlates positively with motivation to excel can be ascribed to the perceived benefits of competition • That is, when incomes vary appreciably across people, individuals assume that a competitive approach is likely to attract more rewards than a cooperative approach. • Alternatively, both income inequality and motivation to excel could be incited by authoritarian leaders.

Procedure 5: The discussion	Example
	<ul><li>These leaders offer promotions and bonuses only to their favoured employees.</li><li>Authoritarian leaders might also inspire a motivation to excel rather than cooperate, as employees strive to attract the support of these leaders.</li><li>Indeed, during the interviews, participants did concede that leadership behaviour, rather than income inequality, was the main determinant of their own motivation and attitudes.</li></ul>Fred offered various explanations to the other key findings as well. In addition, he tried to explain the unforeseen results. For example:<ul><li>Contrary to the hypotheses, motivation to excel was not significantly associated with distrust.</li><li>Perhaps, when employees are motivated to excel, they are especially driven to impress their colleagues.</li><li>This drive to impress colleagues may sometimes translate into trustworthy behaviour.</li></ul>Finally, Fred planned the conclusion as well:<ul><li>Several limitation of this research need to be considered.</li><li>Motivations are often unconscious.</li><li>Indeed, unconscious motivations are sometimes more likely to affect behaviour that conscious motivations.</li><li>Therefore, participants may not</li></ul>

Procedure 5: The discussion	Example
	have been aware of their motivations, contaminating their responses to some of the questions. • Furthermore, the study was not an experiment, and therefore spurious variables, such as economic climate, cannot be dismissed. • Despite these limitations, the findings are consistent with the premise that organizations should cultivate greater equality in income to improve the wellbeing of their employees.

Procedure 6: The summary or abstract	Example
A summary, sometimes called the abstract, appears at the beginning of a report. In general, this summary includes: • One to three sentences that outline the importance of this research, perhaps recounting an interesting fact, statistic, or controversy. • A sentence that outlines the aim of this research. • A few sentences that detail the method, including the variables that were measured or manipulated. • One or two sentences that describe the key results. • A conclusive sentence, perhaps emphasizing the main implication of this research or a possible recommendation.	Fred constructed a series of bullet points to plan the abstract: • Although income inequality in nations has been shown to correlate with many key social problems, two limitations in this literature have not been resolved. • First, whether income inequality actually causes these problems is still contentious. • Second, whether income inequality within organizations correlates with problems has not been examined extensively. • This study was conducted to examine the sequence of problems that income inequality within organizations may incite. • To investigate this issue, 60 participants completed a

Procedure 6: The summary or abstract	Example
	questionnaire that examines income inequality in organizations, anxiety, distrust, and motivations at work.
	- Furthermore, these individuals participated in interviews, designed to explore these issues in more depth.
	- Overall, income inequality did provoke a motivation to excel rather than cooperate as well as distrust. This distrust correlated with anxiety as well.
	- Consequently, initiatives that curb inequality could enhance the wellbeing of employees.

Procedure 7: The title	Example
The style of titles tends to vary across fields. Most titles, however, include the following features: - The title is fewer than 15 or so words - The title summarizes the key variables, such as the cause, the outcome, the mediators, and the moderators. - Redundant words, such as 'a study of' or 'research into', are obviously omitted. - The title often includes a section before and after a colon. - Sometimes, either before or after the colon, the researcher includes a literary device, such as a rhyme, pun, or alliteration.	Fred considered the title 'The association between inequality of income and quality of life: The mediating role of distrust and motivation to excel'.

Deciding which arguments to include

As the research project evolves, concepts or arguments that seemed relevant earlier are not as significant later. For example, a team of researchers may initially want to examine the effects of inequality in income on productivity. However, as they proceed, they decide to focus on the effect of inequality on wellbeing instead of productivity. The articles they read about productivity, as well as the opinions they formed about this topic, are no longer relevant.

Unfortunately, researchers sometimes feel attached to the concepts they understand or to the opinions they have formed. Consequently, they decide to include these concepts or opinions in the final report. The final report, therefore, includes material that is not relevant to the main themes. This report is rambling rather than crisp. Instead, researchers should abandon any material that is not central to the key research questions.

Research discoveries

Sometimes, people understand some concept well or have dedicated significant time to this concept. In these instances, they are especially likely to feel a sense of attachment, or even loyalty, to these concepts (O'Driscol, Pierce & Coghlan 2006). They feel compelled to include these concepts in the report.

Procedure 1	Example
Researchers should evaluate the relevance of each argument they plan to include. Arguments that are not directly related to the hypotheses or results of this study should be excluded.	Fred had initially planned to demonstrate that procedural justice may moderate or change the relationship between inequality in income and anxiety. However, while he conducted the analyses, he did not assess this possibility. In addition, during the interviews, the issue of justice was not raised by participants. Eventually, Fred decided to drop any reference to fairness and justice.
	After excluding any reference to justice, Fred deliberately left his report on a desk in the classroom.

Procedure 1	Example
	He knew that Barney would read this report...

Chapter 10

Writing and refining the draft

On 19 May 2009, *Today Tonight* reported a story on which chemists offer the cheapest prices. Specifically, the program compared a variety of chemists—such as Pharmacy Online, Chemist Warehouse, Priceline, Coles, and specific retailers—on the costs a specific set of items. Overall, Pharmacy Online was the least expensive followed closely by Chemist Warehouse. Coles was the most expensive followed by Priceline.

Although this report seems compelling, the method is arguably flawed. The price that customers generally pay does not depend only on the average price of items. Instead, the price depends on the capacity of individuals to consider the alternatives suitably and choose effectively.

Identify errors and shortcomings of your draft

Research discoveries

If people focus their attention on the specific details, instead of the overall shape, of some object—like a map or house—their capacity to uncover subtle problems tends to improve. For example, while they read their draft, they can more readily uncover violations of writing principles (e.g. Friedman & Forster 2005).

To illustrate, products that are online are often not as vivid as products that are not online. That is, sometimes the quality of photographs and pictures of products online are inadequate. If products are not vivid, people do not utilize their intuition as well (Lee, Amir & Ariely 2009). They do not reach suitable decisions (Dijksterhuis & van Olden 2006).

They may, for example, purchase items they do not need. Consequently, over time, they spend excessively.

The conclusions that were reached by this program, therefore, were misleading and were not written precisely. How can you ensure you write your arguments and conclusions with precision and accuracy? This chapter offers a series of guidelines that students can follow to improve their writing.

To write effectively, your prose needs to be concise, unambiguous, formal, and engaging. Over the years, scholars have proposed thousands of suggestions and guidelines that writers should follow. Some researchers are unaware of many, if not most, of these suggestions and guidelines. They often violate these principles. This chapter focusses on the 100 most common mistakes.

Procedure 1: Concise writing	Example
Instructors often specify the maximum number of words that students can include in a report. Students who can write concisely, therefore, will often receive the best grades. Their reports will include more arguments, details, and subtleties within the word limit. Besides deleting unnecessary arguments and repetition, to write concisely, you need to: • Delete phrases that are actually redundant. For example, in the sentence, 'in order to arrive on time, I use an alarm clock', the phrase 'in order' is redundant. • Simplify phrases that are actually tautologies. For example, 'temporary loan' is a tautology because all loans, by definition, are temporary • Simplify phrases that are verbose. For example, 'in the near future' could be simplified to 'soon'. • Colons can sometimes be used to reduce the number of words	Fred borrowed a book from the library, called 'Success at university: What they haven't told you'. In Chapter 10, this book listed a long series of redundant phrases. Using the Find function in Microsoft Word, Fred first searched the plan he had written to uncover redundant phrases, including: • 'in order', 'in an attempt', 'as a means' • 'it is noteworthy that', 'needless to say' • 'in number, 'in colour', 'in size', 'a total of' • 'a total of', 'a sum of' He then removed these redundant phrases. Second, he searched his plan to uncover tautologies that can be replaced with concise alternatives, including: • 'aims to examine' can be 'examine' • 'a new innovation' can be 'innovation' • 'briefly summarize' can be

Procedure 1: Concise writing	Example
as well. To improve your capacity to write concisely, study the examples that Fred discovered. Eventually, this skill becomes quite natural.	'summarize' - 'completely dead' can be 'dead' - 'complete opposite' can be 'opposite' - 'completely anonymous' can be 'anonymous' - 'might possibly' can be 'might' - 'might perhaps' can be 'might' - 'in actual fact' can be 'actually' - 'foreign imports' can be 'imports' - 'end result' can be 'result' - 'past history' can be 'history' - 'past achievements' can be 'achievements' - 'postpone until later' can be 'postpone' - 'follow after' can be 'follow' - 'repeat again' can be 'repeat' - 'very unique' can be 'unique' Third, he searched his plan to uncover other phrases that can be expressed in fewer words, such as - 'in the near future' can be 'soon' - 'in the process of' can be 'currently' - 'at the present time' and similar phrases can be 'now' - 'until such as time as' can be 'until' - 'on a daily basis' can be 'daily' - 'during the course of' can be 'while' - 'for the most part' can be 'usually' - 'the majority of' can be 'most' - 'equally as' can be 'as' - 'in the vicinity of' can be 'near'

Procedure 1: Concise writing	Example
	<ul><li>'close proximity to' can be 'near' as well</li><li>'located near' can be 'near'</li><li>'due to the fact that' can be 'because'</li><li>'despite the fact that' can be 'although'</li><li>'in the event that' can be 'if'</li><li>'as a matter of fact' can be 'indeed'</li><li>'give to rise to' can be 'elicit'</li><li>'with regards to' can be 'on' or 'about'</li><li>'with respect to' can be 'on' or 'about' as well</li><li>'there is little doubt that' could be 'probably'</li><li>'arrive at the conclusion' can be 'conclude'</li><li>'by way of' can be 'by'</li><li>'is in a position to' can be 'could'</li><li>'take into account' can be 'consider'</li><li>'as to whether' can be 'whether'</li><li>'has the tendency to' can be 'tends to'</li><li>'has the ability to' can be 'can'</li><li>'has an effect on' can be 'affects'.</li></ul>Similarly, Fred discovered that many sentences with 'there' and 'that' separated by a few words can be condensed. 'There are many organizations that pay executives huge salaries' can be reduced to 'Many organizations pay executives huge salaries'. That is, 'there' and 'that' can often be removed.

Procedure 1: Concise writing	Example
	Furthermore, Fred discovered that colons can sometimes be used to replace several words. For example, consider the sentences 'Industries can be divided into two main categories. These categories include manufacturing and services'. In this instance, 'These categories include' can be replaced by a : or colon—a punctuation mark that often precedes a list.
	Finally, Fred was aware that phrases that are incidental, rather than vital, should obviously be removed. For example, Fred knew that brackets should not be included too often. Usually, the phrase inside a bracket (like this) is incidental and, therefore, should be deleted. Sometimes, the phrase within a bracket is vital and, therefore, should be surrounded by commas or em dashes—which are these symbols—instead of brackets.

Procedure 2: Precise writing	Example
The marks that students receive are, sometimes, not as high as they expected. Often, the examiner has misinterpreted the report slightly and, therefore, underestimated the quality of this work. This problem can be ascribed to the tendency of many students to write ambiguously rather than precisely. Students need to be aware of the phrases and words that can be misinterpreted. They need to replace these phrases and words with more precise alternatives. To improve your	Again, Fred consulted the book called 'Success at university: What they haven't told you'. In Chapter 11, this book listed phrases that often need to be replaced with more precise alternatives. First, Fred realized that he needs to specify more precise quantities, including: • 'a number of' can be 'several', 'many' or even a specific number. • 'lack of' can be 'none of' or 'scarcity of'; otherwise the word 'lack' is ambiguous

Procedure 2: Precise writing	Example
capacity to write precisely, study the examples that Fred discovered.	• 'much' can be 'considerable' or 'some'. Second, Fred discovered that some verbs are vague and ambiguous and, therefore, should be replaced with more precise alternatives. For example: • 'I cannot take this frustration' is ambiguous. The word 'take' can imply adopt', 'pinch', 'accompany', 'bring', 'record', or 'endure'. Instead, Fred decided to replace each instance of the word 'take' or 'took' with a more precise alternative. • Similarly, many other verbs—such as 'get', 'got', 'has', 'have', 'had', 'give', 'gave', 'make', 'made', 'hold', 'held', 'come', 'came', and 'done'—are also ambiguous. • For each of these words, Fred visited the website www.thefreedictionary.com. He entered these words in the box at the top to uncover more precise synonyms. Third, Fred realized that many pronouns, such as 'this', 'these', 'those', 'it', and 'they', can be ambiguous—unless specific nouns are included. To illustrate: 'Researchers have not examined this' can be 'Researchers have not examined this **relationship**'. 'These were included to assess inequality' can be 'These **questions** can were included to assess inequality 'It was administered to assess

Procedure 2: Precise writing	Example
	inequality' can be '**This measure was administered to assess inequality**'. Fourth, Fred realized that some grammatical errors diminish precision. He had read some examples of these errors, and these illustrations enabled Fred to prevent similar mistakes. For example: • Sentences like 'Although smelly, John liked his cat' are ambiguous. This sentence implies that John, and not the cat, is smelly. Fred knew to insert the phrase 'although smelly', called a modifier, immediately before or after the noun it modifies. 'The cat, although smelly, was liked by John' is not ambiguous. • Sentences like 'The theory suggests inequality provokes anxiety' are misleading. Theories—as well as data, research, and studies—are not human and cannot, therefore, perform acts that imply human intentions. 'Suggests', 'helps', 'understands', and many other verbs imply some intention. Instead, the sentences 'The theory implies that inequality provokes anxiety' or 'Proponents of this theory suggest inequality provokes anxiety' are more suitable.

Procedure 3: Formal writing	Example
Reports need to be formal. If reports include too many colloquial	In Chapter 8 of the book 'Success at university: What they haven't told

Procedure 3: Formal writing	Example
phrases, the researchers may seem frivolous rather than thorough, methodical, scientific, and objective. To write formally, the language cannot be clichéd, disrespectful, or ungrammatical. To enhance your capacity to write formally and grammatically, study the examples that Fred discovered.	you', Fred uncovered some guidelines on how to write formally and correctly. First, he learnt how to write respectfully. Specifically: • He avoided sexist words. He replaced 'actress', 'forefather', 'mailmen', 'policemen', and 'stewardess', for example, with 'actor', 'ancestor', 'postal worker', 'police officer', and 'flight attendant' respectively. • He avoided the inclination to reduce people to labels. For example, he replaced labels such as 'Indian people' with 'people of Indian descent' and 'schizophrenics' with 'people diagnosed with schizophrenia'. • Whenever he did want to refer to a specific community, such as Aboriginal people in Australia, he asked members of this community which labels they prefer. Second, he avoided clichés. For example: • 'think outside the box' could be 'think creatively' • 'work like a dog' could be 'work vigorously' • 'tried and true method' could be 'validated method' • 'the man in the street' could be 'a typical person' • 'at the end of the day' could be 'ultimately' • 'the bottom line' could be 'the key conclusion' • 'put it in a nutshell' could be 'to summarize', and

Procedure 3: Formal writing	Example
	- 'to take to the next level' could be 'to advance'. Third, he omitted many contractions, replacing don't, can't, and won't with do not, cannot, and will not. Fourth, Fred was aware that people often confuse similar words, such as: - affect and effect - alternate and alternative - between and among - complement and compliment - farther and further - it's and its - less and fewer - past and passed - principal and principle - proceed and precede - there, their, and they're - weary and wary - which and that - whose and who's - your and you're. Whenever he was unsure which of these words to use, he consulted www.thefreedictionary.com. Fifth, Fred read about common grammatical errors. To illustrate, when people use the word 'whereas' and 'although', they need to compare two things in the same sentence. For example, the sentences 'Average income is unimportant. Whereas variability of income is vital' are incorrect. Average income and variability of income are not compared in the same sentence. In contrast 'Average income is unimportant, whereas

Procedure 3: Formal writing	Example
	variability of income is vital' is correct. Fred, therefore, reread his work to ensure he had not committed this error or other violations. For example:

- Phrases such as 'could of', 'should of', and 'would of' should be 'could have', 'should have', and 'would have'
- The phrase' compromises of' should be 'comprises' or 'consists of'
- The phase' data is' or 'data was' should be 'data are' or 'data were'. That is, the word 'data' is plural.
- Singular pronoun, such as she or he, should be used to represent singular nouns, such as person. The sentence 'If you stare at a person, they may feel uncomfortable' is incorrect. The word 'they' should not be used to represent 'a person'.

Finally, Fred resisted his usual temptation to use quotation marks to excuse unsatisfactory language. Initially, he had written:

- Some people do not 'get it'.

He had, however, placed the words 'get it' in quotation marks, because he felt this phrase was unsuitable and colloquial. Eventually, he realized he should phrase this argument more effectively, writing 'Some people do not understand' instead.

Procedure 4: Balanced writing	Example
Besides writing formally, you need to show balance and impartiality. Exclude sweeping claims or forceful language.	Fred avoided unqualified statements that can readily be challenged. For example: ■ 'These people always' could be 'These people may' or 'These people tend to' ■ 'The fact that' could be 'The observation that' He also omitted forceful terms, such as 'must' or 'should'. These terms have been shown to provoke defensive responses in other people, sometimes called reactance. Similarly, he omitted forceful symbols, including: ■ Exclamation marks ■ Bold font, italicized font, or capital letters that are merely intended to emphasize specific words.

Procedure 5: Punctuation	Example
Writers also need to learn how to use punctuation appropriately; otherwise, their writing is more likely to be ambiguous and misleading.	Fred read over his work to ensure he used punctuation correctly. First, he scrutinized the commas he had used. He knew that commas should be used only to: ■ Separate words in a list of words, such as 'The managers were uncooperative, unsupportive, unstable, and unproductive' or 'Four characteristics were measured: income inequality, anxiety, motivation, and distrust' ■ Enclose or segregate phrases that are either optional or could be shifted to other parts of the sentence, such as 'Government departments, for example,

Procedure 5: Punctuation	Example
	regulate salaries' or 'For example, government departments regulate salaries'. 'For example' could be shifted to various parts of the sentence and, therefore, should be segregated by commas.
	▪ Segregate two independent clauses—that is, sets of words that could be sentences by themselves—if separated by the word 'and', 'but', or other conjunctions. An example is 'Governments departments regulate salaries, and many individuals prefer to work in this sector'.
	Second, he scrutinized the semicolons and colons he used. He knew that semicolons tend to separate independent clauses, such as 'Governments departments regulate salaries; many individuals prefer to work in this sector'. He also knew that colons tend precede an example or clarification, such as:
	▪ Government departments offer employees one key benefit: stability
	Nevertheless, some words override the need to use colons, including 'such as' or 'including'. If these words are included, colons should be deleted. In the sentence 'Four characteristics were measured including: income inequality, anxiety, motivation, and distrust', the colon should be omitted.
	Third, Fred ensured that he had used apostrophes correctly. He knew the main rule: When a noun

Procedure 5: Punctuation	Example
	is singular, the apostrophe precedes the s, such as 'the person's name'. When a noun is plural, the apostrophe follows the s, e.g. 'the participants' names'. But, he was aware of exceptions. For example: • If a singular noun ends in one s, the apostrophe follows this s, and no other s is added, such as 'the ibis' eyes'. • If a plural noun is not formed by merely adding an s—such as children, men, women, and people—the apostrophe precedes the s: 'the children's names'.

Procedure 6: Engaging writing	Example
Besides writing correctly, you should also write enticingly. That is, you need to ensure your writing is engaging and enjoyable to read. To achieve this goal, your arguments should be organized cohesively and expressed with simple words.	To improve his report, Fred ensured that each of his paragraphs focus on one argument only. Furthermore, one sentence in each paragraph, often the first, would summarize this argument, called a topic sentence. These topic sentences should proceed logically. Thus, in the introduction of his report, the topic sentences included: • When income inequality is pronounced, individuals realize their satisfaction with life would improve if they outperformed colleagues. • Because of this realization, employees become more competitive and uncooperative. • Uncooperative employees do not tend to trust one another. • As trust declines, employees

Procedure 6: Engaging writing	Example
	become more vigilant and cautious.
	- This vigilance orients attention to potential complications and, therefore, provokes negative emotions.
	The remainder of each paragraph clarified or verified these topic sentences. After writing his topic sentences, Fred mainly wrote short sentences. Yet, reports that include only short sentences, although easy to read, can seem monotonous. To address this matter, Fred combined some of his shorter sentences to form longer sentences. For example:
	- The sentences 'Income inequality is rife in Australian companies' and 'Income inequality provokes anxiety and depression' could be combined to form one sentence.
	- For example, one sentence, in essence, could be inserted in the other sentence, such as 'Income inequality, although rife in Australian companies, provokes anxiety and depression'.
	- The two sentences could be written sequentially but separated by the word 'and', such as 'Income inequality is rife in Australia and also provokes anxiety and depression'.
	Some long sentences are unwieldy, such as 'Income inequality provokes anxiety and is unlikely to be related to a cooperative mindset but does not allow trust to develop'. Fred changed this sentence to

Procedure 6: Engaging writing	Example
	'Income inequality provokes anxiety, inhibits cooperation, and prevents trust'. In this updated sentence, each item in the series, including:
	▪ 'provokes anxiety',
	▪ 'inhibits cooperation', and
	▪ 'prevents trust'
	shared the same grammar. Specifically, each of these items comprised a verb and then a noun. When each item in a series shares the same grammar, the sentence is not as likely to be unwieldy.

Procedure 7: Controversies	Example
Not all instructors or disciplines share the same preferences. For example, some instructors prefer that you avoid the words 'I' or 'we'. They would prefer you to write 'Income inequality is predicted to increase anxiety' rather than 'I predict that income inequality will increase anxiety'. So, you need to clarify the expectations of your instructors about a variety of matters, including their idiosyncratic preferences.	Fred read the course handbook that was written by his instructor. He discovered the instructor:
	▪ includes a comma before the last 'and' in a list, such as 'method, results, and discussion' rather than 'method, results and discussion'.
	▪ stipulated that abstracts must comprise 150 words or fewer.
	▪ indicated the title and abstract should appear on a separate page. The method, results, and discussion do not need to begin on a new page.
	▪ specified the main heading, such as 'Abstract', 'Introduction', 'Method', 'Results', 'Discussion', and 'References', should appear in a bold font and centred. Subheadings, such as 'Participants' and 'Materials', should appear in a bold font but

Procedure 7: Controversies	Example
	left justified.
	• requested that students avoid split infinitives. An infinitive is a verb preceded by the word 'to', such as 'to analyse' or 'to work'. When a word appears between 'to' and the 'verb', the infinitive is split, such as 'to statistically analyse' or 'to vigorously work'. According to some, this word should be placed later in the sentence, such as 'to analyse the data statistically' or 'to work vigorously'.
	Obviously, Fred ensured that his work conforms to the preferences of his examiner.

Add citations and references

If you would like to be suspended or expelled from a course, your wisest course of action is to plagiarize other work. If you want to pass, however, you need to understand the subtleties of plagiarism.

Procedure 1	Example
Researchers tend to utilize one of three techniques to acknowledge the articles or books they utilized: the Harvard style, endnotes, or footnotes. Your first step is to determine which approach your instructor prefers.	In the course handbook that Fred received, students were explicitly told to use the Harvard style.
For example:	
• If they want you to write the author and date of an article or book in the text, such as '(Smith 2010), they prefer the Harvard style.	
• If they want you to insert a number in the text, such as [1], and then list the corresponding	

Procedure 1	Example
article or book at the end of this report, they prefer the endnote style. • If they want you to insert a number in the text, but then list the corresponding article or book at the end of that page, they prefer the footnote style.	

Procedure 2: Harvard style quotes	Example
If you need to conform to the Harvard style and want to quote a short extract from a book or article, surround this quote with quotation marks. Then, specify the author, year, and page number in brackets. Use quotes, however, only when the precise words are vital.	Fred included only one quote in his report. He wrote: • As researchers have claimed, 'One of the most profound social changes in the United States over the last 40 years has been the growing income inequality among social classes' (Oishi, Kesebir & Diener 2011, pg 1095). He was informed that he is also permitted to specify the authors and year outside the brackets, such as: • As Oishi, Kesebir and Diener (2011) claimed, 'One of the most profound social changes in the United States over the last 40 years has been the growing income inequality among social classes' (p. 1095). Fred did not include any other quotes. He did not feel the precise words that other authors expressed were vital.

Procedure 3: Harvard style paraphrasing	Example
Even if you want to present the ideas, but not the precise words, that another author expressed, you still need to specify the book or article in which you distilled this information. Usually, you cite this book or article just before a full stop or comma. You do not, however, need to specify the page number.	After most of the sentences in his introduction, as well as after some of the sentences in his other sections, Fred included a citation. For example, in the discussion, he wrote: • Despite these discoveries, many people, especially after their assumptions about the world are threatened, feel that inequality is appropriate (Jost & Hunyady 2003). • Other studies have demonstrated that income inequality provokes defensive responses (e.g. Loughnan *et al.* 2011). In this instance, Fred discovered that researchers can include the symbol 'et al' to imply 'and other authors'. When the book or article includes more than six authors, researchers will often use this symbol to conserve space. Similarly, when the book or article includes more than two authors and the source was already cited before, they will also use this symbol. Finally, they will include the symbol 'e.g.' to imply that other books or articles have also expressed this opinion.

Procedure 4: Harvard style reference list	Example
Obviously, if researchers specify only the authors and year, the reader might not be able to locate	In the course handbook that Fred received, students were explicitly told to how to specify books,

Procedure 4: Harvard style reference list	Example
the book or article. Therefore, at the end of a report, in a section called 'References', researchers will present more information about each book or article, such as the title. Indeed, instructors will often specify the precise format that students must follow.	articles, and other sources in the reference section. For books, students were told to specify the authors, year, title, city, and publisher, with punctuation that resembles the following example:

For books, students were told to specify the authors, year, title, city, and publisher, with punctuation that resembles the following example:

Wilkinson, R., & Pickett, K. (2010). *The spirit level: Why equality is better for everyone.* London: Penguin.

For journal articles, students were told to specify the authors, year, title, journal, volume, and page numbers, again with punctuation that resembles the following example:

- Oishi, S., Kesebir, S., & Diener, E. (2011). Income inequality and happiness. *Psychological Science, 22,* 1095-1100.
- Loughnan, S., Kuppens, P., Allik, J., Balazs, K., de Lemus, S., Dumont, K., ...Haslam, N. (2011). Economic inequality is linked to biased self-perception. *Psychological Science, 22,* 1254-1258.

As this example shows, to save space, the symbol ... can be used instead of listing the seventh author onwards. For chapters from books, students were instructed to include the authors of this chapter, year, title of chapter, editors of the overall book, title of the overall book, page numbers, city, and publishers, such as:

- Jost, J. T., Wakslak, C., & Tyler, T. R. (2008). System justification

Procedure 4: Harvard style reference list	Example
	theory and the alleviation of emotional distress: Palliative effects of ideology in an arbitrary social hierarchy and in society. In K. Hegtvedt & J. Clay-Warner (Eds.), Justice: Advances in group processes (Vol. 25, pp. 181-211). Bingley: JAI/Emerald.
	Finally, Fred also included newspapers, Wikipedia entries, and other sources in his report. He was not told precisely how to specify these sources in the reference list. Nevertheless, he knew that he should attempt to include the authors, year, title, and other relevant information, if applicable, such as:
	▪ Smith, A. (2010). Inequality is rampant. The Melbourne Gazette, 15 December, 30.
	▪ Income inequality. (n.d.). In Wikipedia. Retrieved 15 December 2011, from http://en.wikipedia.org/wiki/IncomeInequality.
	Note, the reference that corresponds to a Wikipedia illustrates three key principles. First, the entries are anonymous, and hence the name of authors needs to be replaced with the title of this article. Second, the entry is not written on a particular date; the symbol n.d. is included to denote no date. Finally, because these entries change with time, the date at which the information was retrieved needs to be specified.
	Before submitting his report, Fred

Procedure 4: Harvard style reference list	Example
	then arranged the list alphabetically. That is, he highlighted all these references and then used the AZ ↓ icon in Microsoft Word to arrange these sources from A to Z.

Procedure 5: The endnote approach	Example
In some courses, the instructors prefer the endnote approach. To quote or paraphrase, use the same approach as the Harvard style apart from two exceptions. First, in the text, replace the author, year, and page numbers with a superscript number, such as: • As researchers have claimed, 'One of the most profound social changes in the United States over the last 40 years has been the growing income inequality among social classes'[1.] The numbers should be consecutive. Second, at the end of this report, specify the book or article that corresponds to this number. For quotes, also specify the page number, such as: • 1. Oishi, S., Kesebir, S., & Diener, E. (2011). Income inequality and happiness. *Psychological Science*, 22, pg 1095. If you need to specify this book or article again, you can use a condensed format, such as Oishi, Kesebir, & Diener, Psychological	Fred was not permitted to use this style in his report.

Procedure 5: The endnote approach	Example
Science, 22.	

Procedure 6: The footnote approach	Example
In some courses, the instructors prefer the footnote approach. The footnote approach is the same as the endnote approach, except the details of each book or article are not presented at the end of this report. Instead, these details appear on the same page in which the book or article is cited, on the bottom or foot. To illustrate, if the researcher writes 'One of the most profound social changes in the United States over the last 40 years has been the growing income inequality among social classes'[1.] On the foot of this page will be the sentence '1. Oishi, S., Kesebir, S., & Diener, E. (2011). Income inequality and happiness. *Psychological Science*, 22, pg 1095'.	Fred was not permitted to use this style in his report.

Procedure 7: Consider subtleties	Example
The precise format of these references varies across fields and institutions. Consult your course notes to determine whether you should: ■ Include the doi number at the end of each journal article, such as Oishi, S., Kesebir, S., & Diener, E. (2011). Income	Fred was informed that he did not need to include doi numbers, quotation marks, the symbol vol, or the symbol pp. However, according to his course notes, he was supposed to include the year in brackets. Despite these variations across institutions and fields, Fred knew

Procedure 7: Consider subtleties	Example
inequality and happiness. Psychological Science, 22, 1095-1100. doi: 10.1177/0956797611417262. This doi number appears on the front of each article and is like an ID number. • Insert the year in brackets. • Enclose the title in quotation marks. • Include the symbol vol before the volume numbers and the symbol pp. before the page numbers.	that one principle is universal: Students must not plagiarize. Even when they merely paraphrase another article or book, they must refer to the original authors. Barney had copied Fred's report. But, Barney did not realize that he had copied an earlier draft and not the final report. He did not realize that Fred had deliberately included plagiarized paragraphs in this earlier draft. Consequently, Barney was eventually accused of plagiarism. He failed the course. And he failed to receive a promotion.

References

Alter, AL, Oppenheimer, DM & Zemla, JC 2010, Missing the trees for the forest: A construal level account of the illusion of explanatory depth, *Journal of Personality and Social Psychology*, 99, 436-451.

Baumann, N & Kuhl, J 2005, How to resist temptation: The effects of external control versus autonomy support on self-regulatory dynamics, *Journal of Personality*, 73, 443-470.

Bolte, A, Goschke, T & Kuhl, J 2003, Emotion and intuition: Effects of positive and negative mood on implicit judgments of semantic coherence, *Psychological Science*, 14, 416-421.

Braun, V, & Clarke, V 2006, Using thematic analysis in psychology, *Qualitative Research in Psychology*, 3, 77-101.

Brinol, P, Petty, RE & Barden, J 2007, Happiness versus sadness as a determinant of thought confidence in persuasion: A self-validation analysis, *Journal of Personality and Social Psychology*, 93, 711-727.

Clapham, MM 2001, The effects of affect manipulation and information exposure on divergent thinking, *Creativity Research Journal*, 13, 335-350.

Croyle, RT, Loftus, EF, Barger, SD, Sun, Y, Hart, M & Gettig, J 2006, How well do people recall risk factor test results? Accuracy and bias among cholesterol screening participants, *Health Psychology*, 25, 425-432.

Davidson, A & Moss, SA 2010, The negative side of positive thinking, ARESTA.

Dijksterhuis, A 2004, Think different: The merits of unconscious thought in preference development and decision making, *Journal of Personality and Social Psychology*, 87, 586-598.

Dijksterhuis, A & van Olden, Z 2006, On the benefits of thinking unconsciously: Unconscious thought can increase post-choice satisfaction, *Journal of Experimental Social Psychology*, 42, 627-631.

Friedman, R & Forster, J 2005, Effects of motivational cues on perceptual asymmetry: Implications for creativity and analytical problem solving, *Journal of Personality and Social Psychology*, 88, 263-275.

Gebauer, JE, Riketta, M, Broemer, P & Maio, GR 2008, 'How much do you like your name'? An implicit measure of global self-esteem, *Journal of Experimental Social Psychology*, 44, 1346-1354.

Gorn, GJ, Chattopadhyay, A, Sebgupta, J & Tripathi, S 2004, Waiting for the web: How screen color affects time perception, *Journal of Marketing Research*, 41, 215-225.

Griskevicius, V, Shiota, MN & Nowlis, SM 2010, The many shades of rose-colored glasses: An evolutionary approach to the influence of different positive emotions, *Journal of Consumer Research*, 37, 238-250.

Hardisty, DJ, Johnson, EJ & Weber, EU 2010, A dirty word or a dirty world? Attribute framing, political affiliation, and query theory, *Psychological Science*, 21, 86-92.

Henry, PJ 2009, Low-status compensation: A theory for understanding the role of status in cultures of honor, *Journal of Personality and Social Psychology*, 97, 451-466.

Hilbig, BE 2009, Sad, thus true: Negativity bias in judgments of truth, *Journal of Experimental Social Psychology*, 45, 983-986.

Hirt, ER, Devers, EE & McCrea, SM 2008, I want to be creative: Exploring the role of hedonic contingency theory in the positive mood-cognitive flexibility link, *Journal of Personality and Social Psychology*, 94, 214-230.

Johnson, C, Mullen, B, Carlson, D & Southwick, S 2001, The affective and memorial components of distinctiveness-based illusory correlations, *British Journal of Social Psychology*, 40, 337-358.

Jonas, E, Graupmann, V & Frey, D 2006, The influence of mood on the search for supporting versus conflicting information: Dissonance reduction as a means of mood regulation? *Personality and Social Psychology Bulletin*, 32, 3-15.

Jostmann, NB, Lakens, D & Schubert, TW 2009, Weight as an embodiment of importance, *Psychological Science*, 20, 1169-1174.

Kruglanski, AW & Webster, DM 1991, Group members' reactions to opinion deviates and conformists at varying degrees of proximity to decision deadline and of environmental noise, *Journal of Personality and Social Psychology*, 61, 212-225.

Labroo, AA, Lambotte, S & Zhang, Y 2009, The 'name-ease' effect and its dual impact on importance, *Psychological Science*, 20, 1516-1522.

Lee, L, Amir, O & Ariely, D 2009, In search of homo economicus: Cognitive noise and the role of emotion in preference consistency, *Journal of Consumer Research*, 36, 173-187.

Leonardelli, GJ, Lakin, JL & Arkin, RM 2007, A regulatory focus model of self-evaluation, *Journal of Experimental Social Psychology*, 43, 1002-1009.

Lev-Ari, S & Keysar, B 2010, Why don't we believe non-native speakers? The influence of accent on credibility, *Journal of Experimental Social Psychology*, 46, 1093-1096.

Lilenquist, K, Zhong, C & Galinsky, AD 2010, The smell of virtue: Clean scents promote reciprocity and charity, *Psychological Science*, 21, 381-383.

Maass, A, Ceccarelli, R & Ruden, S 1996, Linguistic intergroup bias: Evidence for in- group-protective motivation, *Journal of Personality and Social Psychology*, 71, 512-526.

Mandel, N & Johnson, EJ 2002, When web pages influence choice: Effects of visual primes on experts and novices, *Journal of Consumer Research*, 29, 235-245.

McCornack, SA & Parks, MR 1986, Deception detection and relationship development: The other side of trust, in ML McLaughlin (ed), *Communication yearbook 9*, Sage, Beverly Hills, CA.

McNiel, JM & Fleeson, W 2006, The causal effects of extraversion on positive affect and neuroticism on negative affect: Manipulating state extraversion and state neuroticism in an experimental approach, *Journal of Research in Personality*, 40, 529-550.

Meeter, M & Nelson, TO 2003, Multiple study trials and judgments of learning, *Acta Psychologica*, 113, 123-132.

Meisenberg, G & Williams, A 2008, Are acquiescent and extreme response styles related to low intelligence and education? *Personality and Individual Differences*, 44, 1539-1550.

Miron-Spektor, E, Gino, F & Argote, L 2011, Paradoxical frames and creative sparks: Enhancing individual creativity through conflict and integration, *Organizational Behavior and Human Decision Processes*, 116, 229-240.

Nelson, LD & Morrison, EL 2005, The symptoms of resource scarcity: Judgments of food and finances influence preferences for potential partners, *Psychological Science*, 16, 167-173.

Nordgren, LF, van der Pligt, J & van Harreveld, F 2006, Visceral drives in retrospect: Explanations about the inaccessible past, *Psychological Science*, 17, 635-640.

Nordhielm, CL 2002, The influence of level of processing on advertising repetition effects, *Journal of Consumer Research*, 29, 371-382.

O'Driscol, MP, Pierce, JL & Coghlan, A 2006, The psychology of ownership: Work environment structure, organizational commitment, and citizenship behaviors, *Group and Organization Management*, 31, 388-416.

Paul, B, Salwen, MB & Dupagne, M 2000, The third-person effect: A meta-analysis of the perceptual hypothesis, *Mass Communication & Society*, 3, 57-85.

Pennebaker, JW & King, LA 1999, Linguistic styles: Language use as an individual difference, *Journal of Personality and Social Psychology*, 77, 1296-1312.

Pieters, R, Baumgartner, H & Bagozzi, R 2006, Biased memory for prior decision making: Evidence from a longitudinal study, *Organizational Behavior and Human Decision Processes*, 99, 1-112.

Pike, C 2002, Exploring the conceptual space of LEGO: Teaching and learning the psychology of creativity, *Psychology, Learning, and Teaching*, 2, 87-94.

Pronin, E, Jacobs, E & Wegner, DM 2008, Psychological effects of thought acceleration, *Emotion*, 8, 597-612.

Pronin, E, Lin, DY & Ross, L 2002, The bias blind spot: Perceptions of bias in self versus others, *Personality and Social Psychology Bulletin*, 28, 369-381.

Pronin, E & Wegner, DM 2006, Manic thinking: Independent effects of thought speed on thought content and mood, *Psychological Science*, 17, 807-815.

Proulx, T & Heine, SJ 2006, Death and black diamonds: Meaning, mortality, and the Meaning Maintenance Model, *Psychological Inquiry*, 17, 309-318.

Raghubir, P & Valenzuela, A 2006, Center-of-inattention. Position biases in decision-making, *Organizational Behavior and Human Decision Processes*, 99, 1-112.

Sherman, DK. & Cohen, JL 2006, The psychology of self-defense: Self-affirmation theory, in MP Zanna (ed.), *Advances in experimental social psychology*, 38, 183-242, Academic Press, San Diego, CA.

Sherman, DK., Nelson, LD, Bunyan, DP, Cohen, GL, Nussbaum, AD & Garcia, J 2009, Affirmed yet unaware: Exploring the role of awareness in the process of self-affirmation, *Journal of Personality and Social Psychology*, 97, 745-764.

Simonsohn, U 2007, Clouds make nerds look good: Field evidence of the impact of incidental factors on decision making, *Journal of Behavioral Decision Making*, 20, 143-152.

Slepian, ML, Weisbuch, M, Rutnick, AM, Newman, LS & Ambady, N 2010, Shedding light on insight: Priming bright ideas, *Journal of Experimental Social Psychology*, 46, 696-700.

Smith, PK., Jostmann, B, Galinsky, A, & van Dijk, WW 2008, Lacking power impairs executive functions, *Psychological Science*, 19, 441-447.

Stapel, DA & Van der Zee, KI 2006, The self salience model of other-to-self effects: Integrating principles of self-enhancement, complementarity, and imitation, *Journal of Personality and Social Psychology*, 90, 258–271.

Tomaka, J, Blascovich, J, Kelsey, RM, & Leitten, CL 1993, Subjective, physiological, and behavioral effects of threat and challenge appraisal, *Journal of Personality and Social Psychology*, 65, 248-260.

Torelli, C & Kaikati, A 2009, Values as predictors of judgments and behaviors: The role of abstract and concrete mindsets, *Journal of Personality and Social Psychology*, 96, 231-247.

Trope, Y & Liberman, N 2003, Temporal construal, *Psychological Review*, 110, 403-421.

Tversky, A & Kahneman, D 1974, Judgment under uncertainty: Heuristics and biases, *Science*, 185, 1124-1131.

Werner, CM, Stoll, R, Birch, P & White, PH 2002, Clinical validation and cognitive elaboration: Signs that encourage sustained recycling, *Basic and Applied Social Psychology*, 24, 185-203.

Wilson, M & Daly, M 2004, Do pretty women inspire men to discount the future? *Biology Letters*, S4, 177-179.

Wilson, T & Gilbert, DT 2003, Affective forecasting, *Advances in Experimental Social Psychology*, 35, 345-411.

Zhong, C, Bohns, VK. & Gino, F 2010, Good lamps are the best police: Darkness increases dishonesty and self-interested behaviour, *Psychological Science*, 21, 311-314.

Zhong, C & DeVoe, SE 2010, You are how you eat: Fast food and impatience, *Psychological Science*, 21, 619-622.

Index